Taking Off

AN ANTHOLOGY OF
PARODIES, SEND-UPS AND IMITATIONS

Edited by
TIM DOWLEY

METHUEN

First published in Great Britain in 1984
by Methuen London Ltd
11 New Fetter Lane, London EC4P 4EE
This anthology Copyright © 1984 by Tim Dowley
Individual contributions © as indicated in Acknowledgements

British Library Cataloguing in Publication Data
Taking off.
  1. Parodies
  I. Dowley, Tim
  827'.91208   PN6231.P3
ISBN 0-413-52840-5

Made and printed in Great Britain
by Hazell Watson & Viney Ltd
Member of the BPCC Group
Aylesbury, Bucks

The definition of parody quoted on page xi is
from the New Webster's English Dictionary,
published by Delair (£14.95) and reproduced by
kind permission of Robson Books Ltd.

CONTENTS

	page
Introduction	xi

The Freedom of the Press — 1
Bunglers Beached   *The Guardian* — 3
Classic Stories in Tabloid Headlines   *Barry Anthony and Tobias Miles* — 4
Agony Uncle   *Eric Idle* — 4
A Doctor Writes: Blinking   *Private Eye* — 4
Leading Article   *Simon Hoggart* — 5
Pop Scene   *Private Eye* — 6
Recruiting Advertisement   *Eric Idle* — 7
The Most Unforgivable Character I Have Ever Met   *David Frost* — 9
Summer Madness   *Monty Python* — 10
Mac – New Bulletin   *Private Eye* — 11
Record Reviews   *Monty Python* — 12
The Gift of Laughter   *N. F. Simpson* — 12
Alone with Nature   *Beachcomber* — 14
The Hackenthorpe Book of Lies   *Monty Python* — 14
The Coming British Revolution   *Roger Woddis* — 15
About Books and Authors   *The Newark Times Book Review* — 15
A Life in the Day   *Private Eye* — 17
Sixteen   *Monty Python* — 18
Paperback Best Sellers   *The Newark Times Book Review* — 18
DIY Envoy in Soccer Probe Marathon   *Michael Frayn* — 20

Easy Reading — 21
African Notebook   *Monty Python* — 23
A Nurse's Dream   *Peter Nichols* — 23
The Adventure of the Two Collaborators   *J. M. Barrie* — 24
It's A Fair Sea Flowing   *J. C. Squire* — 26
Bond Strikes Camp   *Cyril Connolly* — 27
God Give Me Patience   *Maud Gracechurch* — 29

Love's Thorny Crown   *Tony Hendra and Sean Kelly*   29
When I leapt Over Tower Bridge   *J. C. Squire*   30
Maigret at Oxford   *Julian Maclaren Ross*   31
In Which Richard Hannay Seems to Meet Bulldog Drummond . . . .
   Alan Bennett   31
Born to Be Queen   *Private Eye*   34
Greedy Night   *E. C. Bentley*   35
Barbara Cartland Disguises Herself as a Cricket Umpire
   Peter Tinniswood   36
A Ballad   *Guy Wetmore Carryl*   36
Farewell, My Lovely Appetiser   *S. J. Perelman*   37
The Postman Visits Pam Ayres   *Private Eye*   39
Smiley All The Way to The Bank   *Private Eye*   40

Ancient and Modern   43
Hymn   *John Betjeman*   45
Prayer   *Alan Bennett*   46
The Prophet Melchizedek Foreseeth the Coming   *Private Eye*   46
From a Martyr's Journal   *John Harding and John Burrows*   46
Thought for the Day   *Private Eye*   47
The Wassail of Figgy Duff   *Michael Flanders*   47
Take a Pew   *Alan Bennett*   48
O Bloody Bloody Jesus   *Tony Hendra and Sean Kelly*   50

Words and Music   51
Good Times Roll   *Neil Innes*   53
East River Rhapsody   *Julian More*   54
I Hold Your Hand in Mine   *Tom Lehrer*   55
April in Wisconsin   *Julian More*   55
Noël Noël   *Peter Nichols*   56

Read Letters   59
A Poor Correspondent   *Michael Frayn*   61
Letter to Not Yet The Times   *Not Yet The Times*   61
Dear Mr Dickens   *Keith Waterhouse*   62
You Write . . .   *William Donaldson*   63
Official Letter   *Raymond Queneau, tr. Barbara Wright*   64
Letter to the SS Times   *Geoffrey Taylor*   65
Yours Faithfully   *Paul Jennings*   65

Theatres of the Absurd 67
Setting the Scene   *Tom Stoppard* 69
Fragment of a Greek Tragedy   *A. E. Housman* 70
A Tub Called Tractatus   *T. Griffiths* 73
Savonarola Brown   *Max Beerbohm* 74
from Evening Dress Essential   *Paul Bailey* 78
Perseverance   *A. P. Herbert* 79
The Absurdity of Being Dundown   *Alan Bennett* 84
Best of the Edinburgh Fringe   *Punch* 86
Some House-party Maugham   *Angus Wilson* 88
So That's the Way You Like It
    Alan Bennett, Peter Cook, Jonathan Miller and Dudley Moore 91

The Good Guide Guide 95
Travelogue   *Leslie Bricusse, Frederick Raphael and Tony Becher* 97
From The Good Food Guide   *Robert Robinson* 97
Egon Ronay Good People Guide   *Monty Python* 98
Some Country Saws   *Alan Coren* 99
Woodworm Tuesday   *Alan Coren* 99
Rhubarb   *H. F. Ellis* 100
Britain As She Is Visit   *Paul Jennings* 100
More Saws
    Alison Prince, J. A. Smith, R. S. Jaffray, R. Rossetti and Martin Fagg 101
The Consumer's Guide to Religion
    Robert Gillespie and Charles Lewson 102

In the Air 105
The Mouse Problem   *Monty Python* 107
Start the Year with Richard Baker   *Miles Kington* 107
Thought for the Day   *Russell Davies* 109
Lady Minerva Throbing's Country Seat   *Private Eye* 110
The Critics   *N. F. Simpson* 111
Novel-writing Live   *Monty Python* 112
Alan Whicker Investigates a Saviour   *Jim McGuigan* 113
Test Match Special   *Private Eye* 113
First Performance   *John Gould and David Wood* 115
Whinfrey's Last Case   *Terry Jones and Michael Palin* 116
A Strong Wind in the Balearics   *Robert Buckman* 118

Laying Down the Law 121
Rex v. Haddock   *A. P. Herbert* 123
In Layman's Terms   *Myles Na Gopaleen* 126
Whereas   *Michael Frayn* 127
Law Report   *Not Yet The Times* 129

The Hapiest Days of There Lifes 133
Swallowing Amazons   *J. M. Crooks* 135
Christopher Robin Goes Coughety Cough   *Paul Griffin* 135
Little Known Last Moments   *R. M. Robertson* 136
William and the Gang Bang   *Tom Lawrence* 136
You are Old, Father William   *Lewis Carroll* 137
Biggles Comes Through   *Graham Chapman* 138
Another Cautionary Verse   *Foxie* 140
Christmas Afternoon   *Robert Benchley* 140
Five Go Mad In Dorset   *Peter Richardson and Peter Richens* 142

Poetic Licence 145
Remember Lot's Wife   *Stanley J. Sharpless* 147
Keeping Up With Kingsley   *Colin Falck* 147
On Wordsworth   *Hartley Coleridge* 148
The Higher Pantheism in a Nutshell   *A. C. Swinburne* 149
A Melton Mowbray Pork Pie   *Richard le Gallienne* 150
Betjeman, 1984   *Charles Causley* 150
Book Review   *Russell Davies* 151
Ancient Music   *Ezra Pound* 152
February Filldyke   *R. J. P. Hewison* 152
Walt Whitman Retrospectively Addresses Old King Cole
   G. K. Chesterton 153
Old King Cole   *G. K. Chesterton* 153
Chard Whitlow   *Henry Reed* 154
Rondel   *Anon* 155
A Country Fair   *Noël Coward* 155
The Man Who Hangs Head Downwards   *Katharine Whitehorn* 156
After the Library   *Douglas Gibson* 157
From the Spanish Cloister   *G. K. Chesterton* 157
Squeal   *Louis Simpson* 158
After Walter de la Mare   *Kenneth Scott* 159
Place Names of China   *Alan Bennett* 160
Dear Father Christmas   *Russell Davies* 161

Anachronisms   163
Paradise Lost 0–1   *Margaret Rogers*   165
Brontë   *George Simmens*   165
The Fish Demon   *Paul Jennings*   166
Breakfast with Gerard Manley Hopkins   *Anthony Brode*   170

Purely Academic   171
The Socratic Method   *H. F. Ellis*   173
How Your Body Works   *Monty Python*   174
Doing Snogging   *Ross McLeod*   175
The Duchess of Wapping   *Noël Coward*   178
Il Minnestrone   *Robert Benchley*   179
O Felix Culpa!   *Frederick Crews*   180
History of England   *W. C. Sellar and R. J. Yeatman*   182

The Big Screen Seen   185
Balham – Gateway to the South   *Peter Sellers*   187
Aftermyth of War
    Alan Bennett, Peter Cook, Jonathan Miller and Dudley Moore   192
The Little Hut of Enmity   *James Saunders*   193
Clive James Looks at the Cinema   *Monty Python*   197
War   *Peter Richardson and Peter Richens*   198

Prosaic   205
The Sublime and the Ridiculous   *Malcolm Bradbury*   207
From *Too Late*   *E. V. Knox*   209
On Dr Johnson   *Jon Fernside*   209
Scruts   *Max Beerbohm*   209
Tough at the Top   *Malcolm Bradbury*   211
Lawrence Examines the British Museum   *David Lodge*   211
A's Trials   *David Lodge*   212
Cold Comfort Farm   *Stella Gibbons*   215
Mrs Dalloway's Clock   *David Lodge*   216
The Peculiar Bird   *E. V. Knox*   216
George Orwell and the Postal System   *Keith Waterhouse*   218
For Whom the Gong Sounds   *Cornelia Otis Skinner*   221

Partly Political   223
Party Political Speech   *Max Schreiner*   225
Speaking as a Friend of His . . . .   *The Guardian*   225

The Chancellor of the Exchequer   *Barry Cryer*   226
Alexander the Haigiographer   *The Guardian*   227
Christmas Message   *Private Eye*   228
Our Thrills in the Big Dipper   *The Guardian*   228

Strange Meetings   231
Dylan Thomas' *Pride and Prejudice*   *Stanley J. Sharpless*   233
Jane Austen's *Under Milk Wood*   *Laurence Fowler*   233
Robert Lowell's *Tyger*   *T. Griffiths*   234
Death Again   *T. Hope*   234
P. G. Wodehouse's *The Castle*   *T. Griffiths*   235
Joyce à Beckett   *Paul Jennings*   235
Rupert Brooke in the Style of McGonagall   *J. Y. Watson*   238
Hercule Poirot Investigates an Elizabeth Bowen Novel
    I. W. Bailey   238
The Caretaker or Private Life   *Alan Coren*   239
The Hawk in the Gutter   *Robert Baird*   241
An Extravagant Fondness for the Love of Women
    Malcolm Bradbury   242
The Love Song of J. Omar Khayyam   *Roy Fuller*   244

Acknowledgements   247
Index   253

INTRODUCTION

Parody
A writing in which the language and style of an author
or work is closely imitated for comic effect
or in ridicule often with certain
peculiarities greatly heightened or exaggerated.

Webster's English Dictionary

Parodies have often been regarded as a particularly esoteric form of
academic humour – dons' delight, strictly for highbrows. This collection began, several years ago, as an anthology of prose and verse
parody, very much in this slightly precious tradition. However, once I
had plunged through the Eng Lit barrier, I discovered a wealth of
lively material elsewhere, parodying almost every conceivable written
– and even spoken – form of English.

Which is not surprising – at base parody is stimulated by a desire to
puncture pomposity, to thumb the nose at teacher. Hence parodies of
the whole range of establishment figures and organisations: the law, the
church, *The Times*, Shakespeare and even Winnie-the-Pooh.

In making this selection, I have tried to adhere to a fairly strict
definition of 'parody', rejecting burlesque, which uses the original
subject or style merely as a jumping-off point for the humorist's own
purposes, and coarse parodies, which simply throw in a couple of the
original writer's obvious characteristics or catch phrases.

Though parodists delight in demolishing the posturings of the
aesthete, the pundit and the authority figure, parody is essentially a
good-humoured activity, in contrast to satire. The best parodists are
often able authors in their own right, who, in parodying a fellow-
writer, are often paying a back-handed compliment. (A compliment
gracefully accepted by the writer in a few cases: 'Most parodies of
one's own work strike one as very poor. In fact one is apt to think one
could parody oneself much better. (As a matter of fact some critics

have said that I have done so.) But there is one which deserves the success it has had. Henry Reed's *Chard Whitlow*.' T. S. Eliot.)

Since parody is primarily a humorous art, I have rejected examples, however accomplished, which parody writers who are no longer widely read, since their impact would be lost on most readers.

To keep the book to manageable proportions, I have in many instances selected extracts from longer parodies; I hope the resulting pieces retain the flavour and wit of their originals.

TIM DOWLEY

Bunglers Beached

[Shock horror in the San Serriffe Express]

EXCLUSIVE

Expressmen expose racket which hurled whitebait into the news
By Express News squad on the spot: Alistair McDonald, Angus McIntyre, Neil Ferguson, Stuart McFarlane, McFarlane Stewart, Elspeth McKenzie, Angus McDonald, Douglas Ferguson. Special Guest Appearance by Neil Stewart, introducing Elspeth McIntyre. Cigarettes by Du Maurier.

AT LAST the world can now learn – must learn – the truth behind the great whitebait whitewash.

It has taken six months to track down the guilty men. Three more months to track down the guilty women. Nine months more to check it out with the lawyers.

It has been the greatest ever *SS Express* inquiry. Our news squad has travelled 150,000 miles, many of them in motor cars.

The *SS Express* bureau chief in Bodoni drove 170 miles to interview the chief suspect – only to find he was out.

Our investigators have been threatened by desperate men. They have faced methods so vile they cannot be described in a family newspaper. They have been shot at. They have been beaten up. They have been spat upon. And they have been called cissies to their face.

Did they give up? They did not. The *SS Express* now tells these evil men that We are Made of Sterner Stuff.

Flushed from the dark and sordid back alleyways of Bodoni, these heartless felons of the fish world now stand exposed in the pitiless glare of public scorn.

Will it end their sordid trade? Will the black scourge of the wicked whitebait saga be lifted for ever?

Time alone will tell. The *SS Express* never will.

THE GUARDIAN
1 April 1978

Classic Stories in Tabloid Headlines
[Peter Pan]

MYSTERY YOUTH, 57, SNATCHES THREE
Miracle Cure For Girl Flier
Crocodile Bites Man

BARRY ANTHONY

[Macbeth]

RUNAWAY FOREST FELLS PALACE PSYCHOPATH

TOBIAS MILES

Agony Uncle

Dear Dr Kraterburg (and Rita),

I am ashamed of having my sexual problems discussed in front of all these people in articles like this. What should I do?

(Name and address withheld)

Being timid or shy of discussing certain sexual matters, or extremely private functions of the body, is a perfectly natural reaction only in nasty neurotic nervous uptight little freaks like yourself. We recommend that you cease withholding your name and address so that we can bombard you with leaflets advertising our expensive books.

ERIC IDLE
The Rutland Dirty Weekend Book

A Doctor Writes . . .
Blinking

Most normal people experience the phenomenon known as blinking – or *oculocculosis temporalis* to give it its proper medical title – as a regular part of everyday life.

4

What happens is that the patient's eyelids momentarily cover the surface of the eyeball at regular intervals. Normally no discomfort is experienced when blinking occurs and the patient is able to live a normal life, at any rate during waking hours.

At nights when the patient is asleep blinking seldom occurs, and if it does, it is rarely noticed, except by very heavy blinkers. It is only when a blink lasts more than several hours at a stretch that a patient should seek medical advice, as it may well be a symptom of what we doctors call blindness.

PRIVATE EYE

Leading Article
[from the San Serriffe Guardian]

AN UNMISTAKABLE CASE OF DOUBT

All men of goodwill throughout our islands will have been heartened by the words of the Bishop of Bodoni. Yesterday he addressed himself to the rioting which has disfigured the face of our North Island, all too recently our South Island. Here is what the Bishop said: 'We must approach this problem in a spirit of brotherly love, and try to see all sides of the problem.'

Wise words indeed, and words which those who find themselves embroiled in these regrettable events will do well to mark. To appreciate the value of the Bishop's statement we could do worse than contemplate what, given his unique position in our national and spiritual life, he might have said. He might all too easily have called for a spirit of murderous hatred to inform all our actions. He might have roused his flock to contemplate only one side of this many-faceted issue and called for a reign of terror to be used against all those who view matters in a different light. Readers of the *SS Guardian* will recall all too well the unfortunate example set by Bishop Crepitano in the fourteenth century whose unwise words on the subject of the Siennese Secession led directly to the Children's Massacre of 1328, with its regrettable attendant loss of life.

The problem of whether the inhabitants of our North Island spell their name 'Flong' or 'Phlong' is clearly one which vitally affects their closest interests. It would be invidious for this newspaper to express an

5

opinion either way; suffice to say that there are strong arguments both for and against each side. It would equally be a mistake for us not to heed the Bishop's words and to express dogmatic views on the question of the use of violence as a lexicographical weapon. There are men of undoubted judgment and sincerity who may be found to champion each side in this dialectical tourney. In conclusion, let our hope be expressed that, in the final outcome of this unfortunate affair, wiser counsels will be seen to prevail.

SIMON HOGGART
The Guardian 1 April 1978

Pop Scene

INTRODUCING THE TURDS
By Maureen Cleavage

I want you to meet four very young and very exciting Turds.

They're from the new Beat Centre of Rochdale and they're swinging into the charts with their first waxing, 'Chain Stagger'.

Young

Yesterday, I popped into the studio and talked to them.

The Turds are something new. Irreverent, greedy, short and acned, there is a trendy look about them that sets a sixties' pace, as up to date as next year's Courrèges Underwear.

The leader of the group Spiggy Topes explained: 'Actually we don't have a leader. In our eyes all Turds are equal.'

Exciting

Spiggy regards the Turds' success philosophically. 'What I say is I mean about this beat business well I shouldn't think we'll be around in a hundred years' time.'

Spiggy is the lead singer and favours a grainy Bo Diddleyesque style that has the youngsters at shriek pitch excitement.

Pacey

I asked him about the controversial microphone stroking that is the high point of his act. 'Is it in any way sexually orientated?' His reply was revealing: 'Of course it is you idiot dolly. Look are you a virgin or something?'

The Turds like everyone else in the world are classless and horrible. The Turds started at the bottom and are already dominating the thinking of pacey people.

I think the Turds are going to be with us for a long time.

PRIVATE EYE

Recruiting Advertisement

THE TEN MOST ASKED QUESTIONS ABOUT THE ARMY

What's it like in Northern Ireland?
Tough, tiring and often dangerous. And that's just for civilians. However, the training you get beforehand is so thorough that we will ensure that you are fully signed up before you're sent over there. Teamwork of course is vital. And there's the satisfaction of knowing that you're doing an important and worthwhile job as a Professional target.

The usual tour is four months with three days' home leave in the middle to help you stop shaking.

What about bull?
There is now very little bull in the Army. In fact this advert is about the biggest bull you'll get.

Rubbing the fear off your trousers takes about seven or eight minutes a day, and the only other thing that needs washing is your brain, and we'll do that for you.

And haircuts?
Over the past two or three years the more desperate we get the more the rules have been relaxed, to the point where your ears no longer stick out like sore thumbs.

But you can forget any ideas of shoulder length hair. Unless you join the Women's Royal Army.

How tough is Basic Training?
Again, very tough, especially the first six weeks. But at least nobody's shooting at you.

If you can't take it, or you're not good enough, you can always run away.

7

How strict is the Army?

There is discipline, there is drill. But it's all designed to help you stop thinking.

When you're relying on your mates, and they're relying on you there is no room for philosophy, or books, or leading a decent life.

If you're not prepared to accept the rules, you're better off where you are. Or where we are. In a nice warm office writing recruiting ads.

Do I commit myself by going to an Army Careers Information Office?

No. You only commit yourself by going to a hospital and becoming a voluntary mental patient.

In fact you might consider doing that rather than joining the Army. Some of the wards are as tough, but on the whole you'll meet a gentler and saner class of person.

Why is the Army still recruiting when soldiers are being made redundant?

The Army is an organisation that needs a continual flow of fit, young men to turn into fine young stiffs.

To achieve this some older men will write almost anything in the adverts for a good compensation and a chance to leave early.

Can I choose any Army job?

Yes, you can choose any job you like. Chances are you won't get it, but you have an absolutely free choice.

What we like to do is show you all our careers at a Selection Centre. Then sign you up and send you to Northern Ireland.

Is there still much travel?

You'll get to see some of the exciting places in the world, provided you keep your head down.

Norway, France, Denmark and Canada are all on the map. Why don't you go there instead?

What's it like to get killed in the Army?

Much better than simply being wounded, which can hurt like hell. Plus you get a decent military burial and a chance to appear on your local war memorial.

Any other questions? If you have any just send them to us. It's not easy to write ads like this that'll fool the unemployed school leaver. Just look in at your nearest Army Careers Information Office and look out. Or post the coupon to THE PROFESSIONAL ADVERTISERS.

ERIC IDLE
The Rutland Dirty Weekend Book

The Most Unforgivable Character I Have Ever Met
By Bob Schulz
[after Reader's Digest]

The train moved slowly over the Rockies. My only companion was a tall man, with grey hair and ears that seemed to glow as we went through tunnels.

Gradually my attention was drawn towards him.

'Nice train we've got here,' I remarked.

'Life is like a railway engine,' he replied.

'Yes,' I said.

'Keep to the rails and you'll reach the everlasting junction,' he rejoined.

By now my eyes were riveted on this strange and compelling figure. But he did not seem to mind.

'Who sleeps with a blind man, awakes cock-eyed,' he mused.

I nodded thoughtfully. Was it really my good fortune to meet a man whose words were imbued with such wit and wisdom? I pinched myself to see if it was true. It was. I waited. Soon, as I had hoped, he spoke again.

'The ant is a busy insect,' he reflected, 'but he still has time to go on picnics.'

'What?' I ejaculated.

'A woman is like a glove – you can put her on and take her off,' he gibed.

'Ah,' I chuckled.

'That's not true,' he conceded.

'It's not,' I breathed.

'No,' he parried.

'Why?' I prompted.

'Because,' he asserted.

9

'What?' I spluttered.

'Yes,' he grunted.

'Oh,' I muttered.

'The rumba is a means of waving goodbye without using the hands,' he quipped.

'Yes,' I voiced.

'Have you no more to say?' he enquired, gazing at me intently with those disconcertingly clear blue eyes.

'Well, I did wonder what made you think of the rumba,' I mumbled.

'Dogs bark, but the caravan goes on,' he chaffed.

'You mean,' I started.

'The caterpillar is just an upholstered worm,' he lampooned.

'Now I see where you're going,' I suddenly disclosed.

'You see?' he demanded.

'I do,' I nodded.

'Sure,' he rumbled.

'Yes,' I purred.

'Where?' he thundered.

'Well,' I faltered.

'What?' he exploded.

I never saw him again. But I see now that I must never forgive him. I must never forgive him for he was unforgivable.

DAVID FROST

Summer Madness
Short story by Elaine Gibson

The story so far: *For the past seventeen weeks Janet has been on a fantastic package tour to Malaga trying to forget Ron, tall blonde photographer's assistant, whom she thinks is having an affair with Olga, her vivacious Russian flatmate. On the beach at Torremolinos (Spain) summer romance has caught up with her in the shape of Renaldo, a hairy wop waiter from the local café. Beguiled by her English freshness, Renaldo has asked her to spend the night with him on some rush matting behind the Spanish National Tourist Office, but she can't help thinking of Ron and wondering where he is.* **Now read on.**

Tenderly Renaldo took me in his arms and pressed his hot Italian lips into my reluctant Reigate ear.

'Now, now, Cherie,' he murmured, his warm body responding roughly to my gentle caresses. But it wasn't Renaldo who occupied my thoughts. My mind and body cried out only for Ron, Ron, Ron. When I thought of those intimate moments in his dusty darkroom as our relationship developed I could hardly believe the evidence of the photographs I'd found. Had that really been Olga? It was hard to tell on those grainy prints, with her face so far away from the camera . . . .

MONTY PYTHON
The Brand New Monty Python Papperbok

Mac — New Bulletin

HE'S OK
SATISFACTORY!!!
Yes, the prime minister's condition is 'Satisfactory' – and that's official!

Mr Macmillan was stated last night to be 'satisfactory' after an operation had been carried out on his moustache. Tension mounted all day outside the Basingstoke County and General Hospital as vast crowds gathered anxiously in the forecourt – crowds of photographers and newsreel cameramen anxiously jostling for shots of the seventh-floor window behind which the full drama of the Prime Minister's operation was being enacted.

From time to time one could see a nurse passing the window, in full nurse's uniform of white cap, starched apron and blue dress. From time to time one could see her pass back again.

Behind the window was the hint of a curtain, of a sort of gauze material, and, looking bravely out on the dramatic scene – a single drooping aspidistra.

Get well messages to the Prime Minister had been pouring in all day from world leaders past and present – such as Chancellor Adenauer, Sir Winston Churchill, and President Eisenhower.

The Prime Minister arrived at the hospital yesterday in a horse-drawn vehicle. Crowds gathered round the entrance as he was carried into the operating theatre, shouting 'Get well Mac' and other encouraging slogans.

Fears in the medical profession that the mange which had attacked Mr Macmillan's moustache might have spread to his brain are now lessening.

Early this morning he was reported as having sat up and asked for chicken and The Earl of Home sat with him for several hours.

PRIVATE EYE

Record Reviews

'Honey you smell' sings Butch on his latest LP 'Feelings'. One knows what he means. Great to hear Flab back in form with their new waxing 'Internal Protection During the Difficult Time'. Salem Records are giving away deodorants with their new singles. Great idea.

MONTY PYTHON
The Brand New Monty Python Papperbok

The Gift Of Laughter
[*Reader's Digest* circa 1955]

Laughter is something we can all indulge in. It is not a gift reserved for the favoured few. But unless our laughter is to be mere empty hilarity, without aim or purpose, we must learn how to use it effectively. How many people know, for instance, that it was an ordinary laugh which could well have been responsible for inflicting on the Russians one of the most devastating diplomatic defeats of the Cold War?

The story, which is quite true except for the facts, begins in 1954 when a well-known frogman, working for NATO, was suddenly suspected for no particular reason of Communist sympathies. Alarmed, he went for a check-up, but the X-ray revealed nothing and eventually the suspicions themselves disappeared. The stigma, however, remained.

A year or so later, an urgent call went out for experienced frogmen to be trained to laugh under water. Among the first to volunteer was the frogman who had been suspected less than two years before of Communist sympathies. He was auditioned, accepted and sent for training. Six months later, and dripping wet, he was passed out. He could now, to use his own words, 'laugh like a gold-plated gridiron' at fifty fathoms.

Then the real test came. He was sent to the seabed off Vancouver Island with orders to laugh – not like a gold-plated gridiron, but like an empty cement-mixer out of control. He did so. The laugh was then picked up sixteen thousand miles away on a privately-owned radar screen, deliberately mistaken for the barking of a seal trapped under an ice-floe in the Bering Straits, hurriedly dubbed into Russian by a team of six plain-clothes Egyptologists from the Sorbonne working round the clock, and re-transmitted on 26,000 megacycles in the direction of one of Soviet Russia's most powerful radio receiving stations.

It was a boldly conceived plan, calling for a high degree of coordination and for split-second timing. Had the Russians mistaken the sound not for the barking of seals, but for the barking of *dogs;* and had they deduced from this that the security forces of the West were engaged in training French poodles to act as underwater bloodhounds somewhere off Nova Scotia, as it was intended they should, they would have been compelled at all costs to devise immediate and effective counter-measures. Counter-measures which could well have involved diverting vital manpower from essential industries in order to experiment with yaks, which were the nearest the Russians could come at that time to experimenting with poodles. Such a disorientation of the Soviet economy at that particular time would have constituted a major victory not only for the West, but for the frogman upon whose laugh the success of the whole enterprise would have depended.

The opportunity to laugh effectively at this level does not admittedly come to all of us every day. But how many of us would be ready to rise to the challenge if it did? How many of us, rather, would find that we had squandered the precious gift of laughter on things that were comic without being in any real sense important? And yet it is today more than ever that we need to recognise the necessity of disciplining ourselves – so that, whether in the struggle against Communism or in some other less spectacular way, our laughter is ready to play its part if ever the need should arise.

N. F. SIMPSON
Harry Bleachbaker

Alone With Nature

What is this nurbling sound under the eaves? It is the tiny quagfinch, lured from his nest in the old juniper by this burst of sunshine. By hedge and ditch nature is leading forth the buds that will later burgeon, as burgeon they must.

Already the stream side is dotted with clusters of upadiddle and old man's foot, and the curious may find in crannies of old walls the lovely bedsoxia, with its trailing stamen and its inverted corolla.

This is the time to pot out your teazle. As the days lengthen and the sun gathers force winged songsters return to the garden – early among them the greater huffle whose red legs terrify the heron so much.

Raspberries should be mulched a little now.

BEACHCOMBER

The Hackenthorpe Book of Lies

Did you know . . .

That El Greco's real name was E.L. Grecott?

Chuck Berry wrote many of Shakespeare's plays?

The Everly Brothers turned down a knighthood?

The Hackenthorpe Book of Lies contains over sixty million untrue facts and figures.

* Did you know that the reason why windows steam up in cold weather is because of all the fish in the atmosphere?

* Did you know that Moslems are forbidden to eat glass?

* Did you know that the oldest rock in the world is the famous Hackenthorpe Rock, in North Ealing, which is two trillion years old?

* Did you know that Milton was a woman?

* Did you know that from the top of the Prudential Assurance Building in Bromley you can see eight continents?

* Did you know that the highest point in the world is only eight foot?

******These are just a few of the totally inaccurate facts in* The Hackenthorpe Book of Lies.

MONTY PYTHON
The Brand New Monty Python Papperbok

The Coming British Revolution

FULL MARX TO STUDENT SANDRA

You wouldn't exactly describe Sandra Pokeworth as revolting, would you? But this shapely young guerrilla fighter (36-22-34) is one of the students who have brought revolution to Britain.

We vote her the Comrade We Would Most Like To Form A United Front With.

So the country's in the throes of a social upheaval. With girls like Sandra doing the upheaving – who's complaining?

Eighteen-year-old Sandra, who hails from the city of Bristol (where else?), came to Whitehall yesterday for a direct confrontation with the Establishment. Lucky Establishment!

Everybody's talking about workers' control. Strikes us the workers will need controlling when they get a load of this piece of property. Hands off, brothers!

Sandra says she's out to change the social structure from top to bottom. Hers looks pretty good to us, the way it is.

ROGER WODDIS

About Books and Authors
By Ned McPeg

DOPPELGÄNGER

A recent note complains that William Shakespeare, not someone else named William Shakespeare, wrote *The Tempest*, which was cited here some years ago as one of several plays printed in the sixteenth century that is still in print. Mr Shakespeare did indeed write a play of the same name, but he, or someone else named William Shakespeare, also wrote *Hamlet* and several other plays.

Plays and books with the same author are not uncommon. *Portrait of the Artist as a Young Man* was written by James Joyce, of course, but so was *Ulysses*. John Jakes wrote *The Bastard,* but his name appears on several other books still in print. Isaac Asimov has written over 200 books and his name appears on all of them.

For Whom the Bell Tolls is by Ernest Hemingway, but so is *A Farewell to Arms,* which also has the name Ernest Hemingway on its cover. *Look Homeward Angel* was written by a young man named Thomas Wolfe, but if you'll check your local library, you'll see several other titles with the same name on them. There would be even more, but Thomas Wolfe died at an early age.

'You can have the same author for different books, for different plays and for different movies, but you're usually more aware of television script writers because they get wider dissemination,' said Beatrix Potter, president of the New York publishing firm, Beatrix N. Potter, Inc. 'The test is whether an author's name is the same as another author's name who has written a book, play or movie with the same title. For example, no one can call himself William Makepeace Thackeray and write a book called *Vanity Fair* because everyone would assume he had already written that book and should go on to something else.

'A single author cannot be as prolific as one who has a mate,' said Ms Potter, 'but two single authors, whether they have the same name or not, can produce more than either could alone, providing they're of the opposite sex. Anyone thinking about calling himself Walt Whitman should know that Mr Whitman was of a different persuasion and never had children, but he did write a lot. It is legal for you to call yourself Walt Whitman and have children, and if you happen to write, too, that's fine, providing you know what you're writing about.'

THE NEWARK TIMES BOOK REVIEW

A Life in the Day
As told to Malcolm Muggerishkyn

A LIFE IN THE DAY OF GOD

Staying awake as I do all the time, I have always found it very difficult to go to sleep. Nevertheless, when I get up, the first thing I like to do is to read *The Times*. I turn at once to the obituaries, to see who I should be expecting for lunch. Last week, for instance, I had Pope Paul VI, Victor Silvester and Doris Waters, a lively lady, who kept us all amused with her tales of a life spent in what I gather is called show-business.

After breakfast, I potter down into my study, a modest little room occupying only four galaxies, and constructed of onyx, chalcedony and some agreeable little clouds, designed by Signor Tiepolo. I cannot wait to hear what Lord Clark has to say about them when he gets up here – if he does!

I spend the morning listening to messages that have been left over-night on the Ansaphone – mainly appeals for help, guidance and so forth. Thank Myself, there are less of these than there used to be. I am told that I don't have quite the following I used to have!

Someone once said that I move 'in a mysterious way'. I have always thought that of all the things that have been said of me, this is one of the more percipient!

I have never bothered with food, so at lunchtime I just look in on my latest batch of guests to see how they are faring. Today there are only seven of them – I gather that none of the other 27,562,421 applicants were accepted.

Now it is time for me to have my daily visit from the gifted team who are working on plans for my next production – the so-called Day of Judgement. Signor Michelangelo shows me some rough sketches for the opening scenes, when mountains dissolve, oceans boil over and that sort of thing. I am not sure that the background music by Signor Verdi is quite tasteful enough – all that brass! But I have taken quite a shine to a funny little American with a cigar called De Mille, who wanders around saying 'Jeez, this is just the way I thought it would look.'

All in all, it is a pretty lonely business up here, and I sometimes wonder whether it's all worth it. But I like to think I do some good in the world, just by being here.

PRIVATE EYE

Sixteen

Printed & Published by Amalgamated Chemicals Group. Books, Magazines, Medicaments, Property Development, etc.

EDITORIAL

It's great to be a girl! Yessir it's good to be alive and really feminine in today's world of startling discoveries. Just look what modern science has given the young girl of today: internal tampons, vaginal deodorants, beauty aids so you needn't look ugly, personal body fresheners so you needn't smell, slimming pills so you needn't be fat, diet sheets to help you if you are, underarm deodorants to stop you smelling all day, feet cleansers, hair cleaners, the pill, Marc Bolan and the WRAC.

It's certainly up to you girls to do your best with so much going for you. Now you can be cleaner than any woman in history, and you need never be ashamed or frightened that your body is going to smell, providing you continually use the right medicaments. Of course the moaning minnies are claiming that many of these products are harmful and cause skin damage, but then they would, wouldn't they? So just you get round to the shops and spend, spend, spend.

Vera

MONTY PYTHON
The Brand New Monty Python Papperbok

Paperback Best Sellers

1. *An Obese Cat*, by Garfield Large. (Valentine, $5.95.) The current adventures of a fat cat.

2. *Fat Cat Fatter*, by Garfield Large. (Valentine, $5.95.) Tons of humor.

3. *Fat Cat Is Large*, by Garfield Large. (Valentine, $5.95.) More tons of humor.

4. *Fat Cat Is Funny*, by Garfield Large. (Valentine, $5.95.) Even more funny fat.

5. *How To Make A Cat Purr*, by Hyman Wand. (Beatrix N. Potter, $3.95.) Sexy humor.

6. *How To Keep Your Cat Alive*, by Arlo Purr. (Valentine, $7.95.) Serious repair manual for cat owners.

7. *Maidenhead Removed*, by Marilyn Wah. (Small, Tan, $5.95.) Intimate noncat fiction.

8. *Jukebox*, by Guernsey Kentucky. (Purdue, $6.95.) A tone-deaf woman wants to help her executive boyfriend learn to sing: fiction.

9. *You Can Do The Bomb*, by Patricia Berserk. (Penicillin, $1.95.) Instructions by a thirteen-year-old English schoolgirl.

10. *Nuclear Destruction: What Is It?* by The Groundhog Society. (Pickpocket, $2.95.) A humorous look at groundhog shadows cast by the light of a nuclear blast.

11. *Mastering Reagan's Bombs*, by George Brash. (Halt, $1.95.) How to assemble nuclear warheads: American humor.

12. *What Color Is Your Bomb?* by Al Hague. (Five-Speed Press, $7.95.) Guide for distinguishing between silver American bombs and dangerous red Russian bombs.

13. *In Search Of Reagan's Bomb*, by Carrie Trousseau. (Halt, $4.95.) How the President lost a bomb in Arkansas chronicled in cartoons.

14. *The I-Hate Bombs Handbook*, by Ichiro Osada. (Warbaby, $3.95.) A biased view of nuclear war by a Hiroshima victim.

15. *Bomb Play*, by Rosemary Reagan. (Rave On, $4.95.) A film star's daughter plays games with 100 megaton bombs: nonfiction.

THE NEWARK TIMES BOOK REVIEW

Do-It-Yourself Envoy In Soccer Probe Marathon

Rain horror ended Britain's miracle heatwave last night. Millions of viewers saw the man they call Mr X, the mystery man in the Sex-in-the-Snow case, mention the Royal Family on TV.

Mr X – a Mayfair playboy well-known in Café Society and the International Set – will pinpoint the area where shapely brunette 'Mrs Undies' says her wonder hubby sent her to Coventry.

Police with tracker dogs and firemen with breathing apparatus fought to bring the mini-miracle under control.

Thirty-two-year-old hole-in-the-head secrets man 'Mr Showbiz' collapsed after a Dolce-Vita-type milk stout orgy. In a plush night-club doctors struggled desperately to save his life.

But it overpowered them and escaped.

Top scientists threw a cordon round the doomed area. The trapped men retaliated by throwing a drag-net round the scientists, and going through them with a fine-tooth-comb to locate the missing super-horror in a twelve-minute mini-marathon.

MICHAEL FRAYN
The Tin Men

Easy Reading

African Notebook
by Col. B. B. Wakenham-Palsh MC, OBE

CHAPTER 19: A LUCKY ESCAPE

The next day I decided to take my usual pre-breakfast 'stroll', as I used to call it, into the *majambi*, or jungle, to see if I could catch sight of the very rare 'Chukawati Bati' or Bird of Purgatory, which 'Trusty', as we all called our faithful native *ghabi* or guide, had reported seeing the previous *latbani* (evening) while we were looking for Harry's leg.

I had only been 'strolling' along the *majambi* (jungle) *ortobam* (path) for a few minutes when I became aware of a large and rather fierce *fritbangowonkabwaki*, or lion, which was standing partially hidden in the *pteee*, or clearing. I had strayed so close to him, absorbed as I was in my ornithological *questi* (quest) that when the splendid old thing opened its massive *goti* (jaws) to roar, revealing as fine a *womba*, or set, of teeth as I have seen in an adult male, each one as *bewapsiptoof'tag* (sharp) as a Welshman's head, I could, without so much as leaning forward, have taken his magnificent uvula in my left hand. Taking advantage of my good luck, I did so, tweaked it hard, an old English colonial officer's *granwi*, or trick . . . .

MONTY PYTHON
The Brand New Monty Python Papperbok

A Nurse's Dream

BARNET. Her bedside alarm gave raucous tongue and Staff Nurse Cleo Norton awoke mid-afternoon suddenly, bewilderingly, and some moments passed before she could realise she was in her room at the nurses' residential hostel . . . .

Her tousled hair and the rumpled sheets were evidence enough of a fitful sleep. If evidence she needed! She flounced over in bed, flung back the sheets petulantly and swung her lithe coffee-coloured legs

23

round till her feet touched the pretty coconut mat she brought from Jamaica all those years ago.

Stretching langorously, she reached for her housecoat and wrapped it demurely around her trim figure . . . .

Outside, the same breeze was still sending newly-laundered white clouds scudding across the blue, like members of a *corps de ballet* obeying the behest of some unseen choreographer. Suddenly nauseated, she flung herself on the bed.

STAFF. What's the matter with you anyway, Cleo Norton?

BARNET. – she demanded of herself, half angrily. But the mad ecstatic leap of her heart had already told her.

STAFF. Neil!

BARNET. In the submarine strangeness of the night ward, young Doctor Neil Boyd's fingers had fleetingly touched hers. And his usually stern features had crumpled into a yearning smile. Their eyes had met and ricocheted away . . . .

PETER NICHOLS
The National Health

The Adventure of the Two Collaborators

In bringing to a close the adventures of my friend Sherlock Holmes I am perforce reminded that he never, save on the occasion which, as you will now hear, brought his singular career to an end, consented to act in any mystery which was concerned with persons who made a livelihood by their pen. 'I am not particular about the people I mix among for business purposes,' he would say, 'but at literary characters I draw the line.'

We were in our rooms in Baker Street one evening. I was (I remember) by the centre table writing out 'The Adventure of the Man without a Cork Leg' (which had so puzzled the Royal Society and all the other scientific bodies of Europe), and Holmes was amusing himself with a little revolver practice. It was his custom of a summer evening to fire round my head, just shaving my face, until he had made a photograph of me on the opposite wall, and it is a slight proof of his skill that many of these portraits in pistol shots are considered admirable likenesses.

I happened to look out of the window, and perceiving two gentlemen advancing rapidly along Baker Street asked him who they were. He immediately lit his pipe, and, twisting himself on a chair into the figure eight, replied:

'They are two collaborators in comic opera, and their play has not been a triumph.'

I sprang from my chair to the ceiling in amazement, and he then explained:

'My dear Watson, they are obviously men who follow some low calling. That much even you should be able to read in their faces. Those little pieces of blue paper which they fling angrily from them are Durrant's Press Notices. Of these they have obviously hundreds about their person (see how their pockets bulge). They would not dance on them if they were pleasant reading.' . . .

Up I went to the ceiling, and when I returned the strangers were in the room.

'I perceive, gentlemen,' said Mr Sherlock Holmes, 'that you are at present afflicted by an extraordinary novelty.'

The handsomer of our visitors asked in amazement how he knew this, but the big one only scowled.

'You forget that you wear a ring on your fourth finger,' replied Mr Holmes calmly.

I was about to jump to the ceiling when the big brute interposed.

'That Tommy-rot is all very well for the public, Holmes,' said he, 'but you can drop it before me. And, Watson, if you go up to the ceiling again I shall make you stay there.'

Here I observed a curious phenomenon. My friend Sherlock Holmes *shrank*. He became small before my eyes. I looked longingly at the ceiling, but dared not.

'Let us cut the first four pages,' said the big man, 'and proceed to business. I want to know why –'

'Allow me,' said Mr Holmes, with some of his old courage. 'You want to know why the public does not go to your opera.'

'Exactly,' said the other ironically, 'as you perceive by my shirt stud.' He added more gravely, 'And as you can only find out in one way I must insist on your witnessing an entire performance of the piece.'

25

It was an anxious moment for me. I shuddered, for I knew that if Holmes went I should have to go with him. But my friend had a heart of gold. 'Never,' he cried fiercely, 'I will do anything for you save that.'

'Your continued existence depends on it,' said the big man menacingly.

'I would rather melt into air,' replied Holmes, proudly taking another chair. 'But I can tell you why the public don't go to your piece without sitting the thing out myself.'

'Why?'

'Because,' replied Holmes calmly, 'they prefer to stay away.' . . .

J.M. BARRIE

It's a Fair Sea Flowing
[after Sir Henry Newbolt]

It was eight bells in the forenoon and hammocks
    running sleek
  (*It's a fair sea flowing from the West*),
When the little Commodore came a-sailing up the
    Creek
  (*Heave Ho! I think you'll know the rest*),
Thunder in the halyards and horses leaping high,
Blake and Drake and Nelson are listenin' where
    they lie,
Four and twenty blackbirds a-bakin' in a pie,
  And the *Pegasus* came waltzing from the West.

Now the little Commodore sat steady on his keel
  (*It's a fair sea flowing from the West*),
A heart as stout as concrete reinforced with steel
  (*Heave Ho! I think you'll know the rest*).
Swinging are the scuppers, hark, the rudder snores,
Plugging at the Frenchmen, downing 'em by scores.
Porto Rico, Vera Cruz, and also the Azores,
  And the *Pegasus* came waltzing from the West.

26

So three cheers more for the little Commodore
  (*It's a fair sea flowing from the West*),
I tell you so again as I've told you so before
  (*Heigh Ho! I think you know the rest*).
Aged is the Motherland, old but she is young
(Easy with the tackle there – don't release the bung),
And I sang a song like all the songs that I have ever
    sung
  When the *Pegasus* came sailing from the West.

J.C. SQUIRE

Bond Strikes Camp

[007 is ordered into drag to trap General Count Apraxin]

Bond consulted the address of his next 'armourer'. It was a studio off Kinnerton Street. The musical cough of the Pierce Arrow was hardly silent when the door was opened by a calm young man who looked him quickly up and down. Bond was wearing one of his many pheasant's-eye alpacas which exaggerated the new vertical line – single-breasted, narrow lapels, ton-up trousers with no turn-ups, peccary suede shoes. A short covert-coat in cavalry twill, a black sting-ray tail of a tie, an unexpected width of shoulder above the tapering waist and the casual arrogance of his comma of dark hair low over the forehead under his little green piglet of a hat completed the picture of mid-century masculinity. The young man seemed unimpressed. 'Well, well, how butch can you get? You've left it rather late. But we'll see what we can do.'

He turned Bond towards the lighted north window and studied him carefully, then he gave the comma a tweak. 'I like the spit-curl, Gerda, we'll build up round that. Now go in there and strip.'

When he came out in his pants, the barracuda scars dark against the tan, a plain girl was waiting in a nurse's uniform. 'Lie down, Gerda, and leave it all to Miss Haslip,' said the young man. She stepped forward and began, expertly, to shave his legs and armpits. 'First a shave, then the depilatory – I'm afraid, what with the fittings, you'll be here most of the day.' It was indeed one bitch of a morning. The only consolation was that the young man (his name was Colin Mount) allowed him to keep the hair on his chest. 'After all, nobody wants you *all* sugar.'

After the manicure, pedicure and plucking of the eyebrows it was time to start rebuilding. Bond was given a jock-strap to contain his genitals; the fitting of an elaborate chestnut wig so as to allow the comma to escape under it was another slow process. And then the artificial eye-lashes. Finally what looked like a box of tennis balls was produced from a drawer. 'Ever seen these before?'

'Good God, what *are* they?'

'The very latest in falsies – foam-rubber, with electronic self-erecting nipples – pink for blondes, brown for brunettes. The things they think of! Which will you be? It's an important decision.'

'What the hell do I care?'

'On the whole I think you'd better be a brunette. It goes with the eyes. And with your height we want them rather large. Round or pear-shaped?'

'Round, for Christ's sake.'

'Sure you're not making a mistake?'

The falsies were attached by a rubber strap, like a brassière, which – in black moiré – was then skilfully fitted over them. 'How does that feel? There should be room for a guy to get his hand up under the bra and have a good riffle.' Then came the slinky black lace panties and finally the black satin evening skirt with crimson silk blouse suspended low on the shoulder, a blue mink scarf over all and then the sheerest black stockings and black shoes with red stilettos. Bond surveyed himself in the long glass and experienced an unexpected thrill of excitement; there was no doubt he had a damned good figure . . . .

CYRIL CONNOLLY

God Give Me Patience

To help us on life's busy road, a road both steep and long, a draught so
fine that will revive is cordial Patience Strong. Too long has she
rejected been, too long bethought as square; now of her splendid poesy
have we become aware. For we've re-found her noble verse, re-learnt
her wisdom fine, her genteel way of saving space, and her language,
rich as wine. Her verses show life's weft and woof, both in sunshine
and in showers, the sparkling dew upon the grass, the birds and bees
and flowers. O, let us now praise Penguin books, who offer us this
crown, this diadem of priceless pearls, as light as thistledown. So let's in
triumph glasses raise and hymn in happy song the poets of great
England's prime: Will Shakespeare and Miss Strong.

MAUD GRACECHURCH

Love's Thorny Crown

Gethsemane. I was only a girl still, although already blooming with the
promise of a woman's lushness, when I first heard the name of the place
spoken. Gethsemane! Even then, my slender frame trembled at the
sound of the word, with its deep overtones of night, torch light, and
flashing swords, while my cheeks warmed and reddened to its sweet
angelic harmonies of tears, and pain, and Love Everlasting.

Little did I think then, that one dark and dangerous night, I would
be *there,* with *Him,* in Gethsemane . . . .

'Mary! Mary Magdalene! You come down here, girl, and get to
work!' My reveries were shattered by this harsh but shrill voice. I had
been gazing dreamily out the window, at the busy streets and quiet
hills of my native city, Jerusalem. It was a beautiful April morning, in
the year 33 A.D. . . .

I had been born to haughty and aristocratic parents in Galilee, in
Magdala, the town which yet bears our ancient family name. But all
that we possessed, including the lives of my dear parents, had been lost
in the bloody rebellion of the two Rabbis Judah and Mattathias, who
ten years before had endeavoured to remove from above the Temple
gate the Roman eagle which they regarded as a symbol of idolatry.
Both they and their suspected sympathisers were slaughtered.

29

Thus, at a tender age, I had to make my way alone in the world, and found employment in a capacity which I considered beneath my proud station, yet not altogether unworthy (for it is a saying among my people that 'A young woman must eat'). It was an occupation my magnificent light-brown long hair made me ideally suited for. I was a foot anointer.

Madam Judith, the ribald but kind-hearted old woman who served as my landlady and employer, had prepared for me the customary alabaster box of costly spikenard ointment, and now gave me directions to the house where the anointing was to be given.

It was in Bethany, a suburb situated a mile and a half away, outside the walls of Jerusalem, she said. So. An out-of-town job. 'At the home,' she added, 'of Simon the Leper'.

'You know I don't do lepers,' I shouted, indignantly . . . .

TONY HENDRA AND SEAN KELLY
Not the Bible

When I Leapt Over Tower Bridge
[A ballad of Chestertonian whimsy]

When I leapt over Tower Bridge
  There were three that watched below,
A bald man and a hairy man,
  And a man like Ikey Mo.

When I leapt over London Bridge
  They quailed to see my tears,
As terrible as a shaken sword
  And many shining spears.

But when I leapt over Blackfriars
  The pigeons on St Paul's
Grew ghastly white as they saw the sight
  Like an awful sun that falls;

And all along from Ludgate
  To the wonder of Charing Cross,
The devil flew through a host of hearts –
  A messenger of loss.

With a rumour of ghostly things that pass
With a thunderous pennon of pain,
To a land where the sky is as red as the grass
And the sun as green as the rain.

J. C. SQUIRE

Maigret at Oxford
[translated from the French, Maigret chez les Dons*]*

Maigret emerged into the street again and mopped his forehead. It was
a hot morning for England. The sun shone here, it seemed, same as
anywhere else! He took a glass of beer from his pocket and drained it
gratefully. Nowadays he always carried two or three about with him,
ever since he'd been caught short by this barbarous British custom, that
they called *les lois de licence,* or, more familiarly, *ouverture et fermeture
temps.*

But – hang on! – he'd misjudged the country after all. *Ils* were open
already – here was a door swinging wide on a smell of *ale,* as though to
welcome him in . . . .

Le publique comptoir. Tables. Wooden benches round the walls. A
board for the *jeu de dards.* Empty except for himself and the *gouverneur*
in shirt-sleeves awaiting his order by the sandwiches under a glass
dome.

'*Police Judiciaire!*' growled Maigret. '*Bière!*' . . .

JULIAN MACLAREN ROSS

In Which Richard Hannay Seems to Meet Bulldog Drummond . . . .

SANDY CLANROYDEN. Ned. Did you ever hear of a man called
George Ampersand?

LEITHEN. Bostonian philanti opist and friend of kings! Who hasn't?

SANDY. I had some talk with Mr Baldwin this morning. I never saw a
man more worried.

31

HANNAY. Of late, Ned, there have been a succession of small disasters, oh trifling in themselves . . . a Foreign Secretary's sudden attack of dysentery at the funeral of George V, an American ambassador found strangled in his own gym-slip, and in Sudetenland, most mysterious of all, a Laughing Leper who destroys whole villages with his infectious giggles.

SANDY. The tide is flowing fast against monarchy in Europe. Scarcely a week passes but a throne falls. Mr Baldwin thinks it may be our turn next.

LEITHEN. Who is behind it all this time?

HANNAY. Who? That poses something of a problem. To the good people of the neighbourhood he is a white-haired old man with a nervous habit of moving his lips as he talks. To the members of a not unfamiliar London club he is our second most successful theologian. But the world knows him as . . . George Ampersand.

LEITHEN. Ampersand. Good God.

HANNAY (*handing him snapshots*). He is surrounded by some of the worst villains in Europe. Irma, his wife. Nature played a cruel trick upon her by giving her a waxed moustache. Sandro, his valet. A cripple of the worst sort, and consumptive into the bargain.

LEITHEN. Is he sane?

SANDY. Sane? He is brilliantly sane. The second sanest in Europe. But like all sane men he has at one time or another crossed that thin bridge that separates lunacy from insanity. And this last week the pace has quickened. Else explain why a highly respected Archbishop of Canterbury, an international hairdresser and a very famous king all decide to take simultaneous holidays on the Black Sea.

HANNAY. Take a look at this snapshot. It's of a simultaneous holiday on the Black Sea.

LEITHEN. But that's . . . .

HANNAY. Exactly. A young man not entirely unconnected with the English throne.

LEITHEN. Who is she?

SANDY. She's beautiful, isn't she? An American. Women are queer cattle at the best of times but she's like no other woman I've ever known. She has all the slim grace of a boy and all the delicacy of a young colt.

LEITHEN. It's a rare combination. Who's this?

HANNAY. Completely Uncrupulos, the Greek shipping magnate.

LEITHEN. He's got himself into a pretty rum set. And yet he looks happy.

HANNAY. That's what Mr Baldwin doesn't like about it. During the past few months certain reports have been appearing in what for want of a better word the Americans call their newspapers.

LEITHEN. About her?

HANNAY. Yes.

LEITHEN. And him?

HANNAY. Yes.

LEITHEN. But . . . I don't understand . . . where lies the difficulty? If he loves her . . . .

HANNAY. I don't think you understand. She is what we in the Church of England called a divorced woman.

LEITHEN. God! It's filthy!

HANNAY. A divorced woman on the throne of the house of Windsor would be a pretty big feather in the cap of that bunch of rootless intellectuals, alien Jews and international pederasts who call themselves the Labour Party.

LEITHEN. Your talk is like a fierce cordial . . . .

ALAN BENNETT
Forty Years On

Born to Be Queen
by Sylvie Krin
[as told to Barbara Cartland]

The story so far: *His Royal Highness Prince Charles is still unmarried at the age of thirty-two. Searching for a suitable bride, his eye lights on lovely nineteen-year-old Lady Diana Spencer.* **Now read on:**

Lady Dartmouth's hands trembled slightly as she picked up the large cream envelope embossed with the Royal Crest which lay on top of her silver breakfast tray.

'What's that you've got there, darling?' came the commanding voice of her mother, the gracious authoress Dame Barbara Cartland who sat at the far end of the table swathed in furs and surrounded by pots of honey and vitamin pills. No wonder, her daughter thought, that even at eighty-four she still made men's heads turn when she shopped for yoghourt in Harrods.

Lady Dartmouth ran a silver paper-knife through the hand-made envelope. Her voice trembling with emotion she read aloud: 'His Royal Highness requests the pleasure of Lady Diana Spencer at Windsor Castle November 29th. Polo and free-fall parachuting. Black tie.'

At that moment the door opened, and four sleek black labradors bounded into the breakfast room followed by the Earl of Spencer wearing his customary smart tweeds and green wellington boots.

'What's up, darling?' he cried, helping himself to kedgeree at the sideboard.

Lady Dartmouth gave her husband a despairing look. 'If you must know,' she said in icy tones, 'your daughter has received an invitation from the Palace. You realise what *that* might mean.'

The Earl took his place at the table and sprinkled royal jelly absent-mindedly on his plate. Sometimes he wished he had never left his former wife to live with Raine. She could be so overbearing. And as for her mother, now firmly established in the spare wing, there were moments when he thought she was a terrible ogre out of a fairy-tale.

His reverie was interrupted by the brush of young lips on his cheek.

'Good morning, papa!' came the soft reassuring voice of his daughter Diana.

'Never mind that you silly child!' her stepmother rasped. 'Look at

34

this! An invitation from the Prince of Wales. You've to spend the weekend with him at Windsor November 29th.'

The innocent young Diana blushed. 'But Raine! That's the weekend of the Young Farmers' Ball! I promised to help with the Tombola.' . . .

PRIVATE EYE

Greedy Night by D*r*thy L. S*y*rs

'Thank you, my lord.' Bunter laid an armful of newspapers on the bed and withdrew. When he returned with the breakfast tray Wimsey was reading with absorbed interest. 'Bunter,' he said eagerly, 'I see that at Sotheby's on Monday they're auctioning a thing I simply must have – the original manuscript of the *Chanson de Roland,* with marginal notes by Saint Louis. If I find I can't go myself, I shall want you to pop round and bid for me. That is, of course, if it's the genuine article. You could make sure of that, I suppose?'

'Without difficulty, my lord. I have always taken an interest in the technical study of mediaeval calligraphy. I should be sceptical, though, about those marginal notes, my lord. It has always been understood, your lordship will recollect, that His Most Christian Majesty was unable to write. However – '

At this point there came a long-continued ringing at the door-bell of the flat; and after a brief interval Bunter, with all the appearance of acting under protest, showed the Bishop of Glastonbury into the bedroom.

'I say, Peter, there's the devil to pay!' exclaimed that prelate. 'Topsy's pretty well off her onion, and Bill Mixer's in a frightful dither. Have you heard what's happened? But, of course, you couldn't. They've been trying to get you on the phone this morning, but that man of yours kept on saying that he feared his lordship was somewhat closely engaged at the moment. So they rang me up and asked me to tell you.'

'Well, why not tell me?' Wimsey snapped. Topsy, the Bishop's favourite sister, was an old friend, and her husband was a man for whom Wimsey had a deep regard that dated from his years at Balliol.

'Dermot's dead.' . . .

E.C. BENTLEY

Barbara Cartland Disguises Herself as a Cricket Umpire

Her reveries were interrupted as a ripple of applause rippled among the spectators whose honest ruddy faces rippled the splintered summer sunlight.

She looked up and her heart missed a beat.

It was him.

No.

It was he.

He strode out to the wicket with that lissom lilt to the limbs, that purposeful manly tread, that ripple of rippling muscles that turned her knees to jelly.

And how her heart fluttered to the jut of his jaw, the straightness of that aristocratic aquiline nose, the haughty glint to those broodingly passionate smouldering eyes that rippled beneath the rippling black of his noble mane.

'Dexter, Dexter,' she breathed to herself.

Now she could feel the juices quicken in her body as he approached the wicket.

Nearer and nearer and nearer he came and then of a sudden he was standing next to her.

In person. . . .

PETER TINNISWOOD
More Tales From a Long Room

A Ballad
[Rudyard K.]

As I was walkin' the jungle round, a-killin' of tigers an' time;
I seed a kind of an author man a writin' a rousin' rhyme;
'E was writin' a mile a minute an' more, an' I sez to 'im, 'oo are you?'
Sez 'e 'I'm a poet – 'er majesty's poet – soldier and sailor, too!'
An 'is poem began in Isfahan an' ended in Kalamazoo,
It 'ad army in it, an' navy in it, an' jungle sprinkled through,
For 'e was a poet – 'er majesty's poet – soldier an' sailor, too.

An' after, I met 'im all over the world, a doin' of things a host;
'E 'ad one foot planted in Burmah, an' one on the Gloucester coast;
'E's 'alf a sailor an' 'alf a whaler, 'e's captain, cook, and crew,
But most a poet – 'er majesty's poet – soldier an' sailor too!
'E's often Scot an' 'e's often not, but 'is work is never through,
For 'e laughs at blame, an' 'e writes for fame, an' a bit for revenoo –
Bein' a poet – 'er majesty's poet – soldier an' sailor too!

'E'll take you up to the Ar'tic zone, 'e'll take you down to the Nile,
'E'll give you a barrack ballad in the Tommy Atkins style,
Or 'e'll sing you a Dipsy Chantey, as the bloomin' bosuns do,
For 'e is a poet – 'er majesty's poet – soldier an' sailor too.
An' there isn't no room for others, an' there's nothin' left to do;
'E 'as sailed the main from the 'Arn to Spain, 'e 'as tramped the jungle
    through
An' written up all there is to write – soldier an' sailor too!

There are manners an' manners of writin', but 'is is the *proper* way,
An' it ain't so hard to be a bard if you'll imitate Rudyard K.;
But sea an' shore an' peace an' war, an' everything else in view –
'E 'as gobbled the lot! – 'er majesty's poet – soldier an' sailor, too.
'E's not content with 'is Indian 'ome, 'e's looking for regions new,
In another year 'e'll 'ave swept 'em clear, 'an what'll the rest of us do?
'E's crowdin' us out! – 'er majesty's poet – soldier an' sailor too!

GUY WETMORE CARRYL

Farewell, My Lovely Appetiser
[after Chandler]

Add Smorgasbits to your ought-to-know department, the newest of the three Betty
Lee products. What in the world! Just small mouth-size pieces of herring and of
pinkish tones. We crossed our heart and promised not to tell the secret of their tinting.
Clementine Paddleford's food column in the Herald Tribune.

    The 'Hush-Hush' Blouse. We're very hush-hush about his name, but the celebrated
shirtmaker who did it for us is famous on two continents for blouses with details like
those deep yoke folds, the wonderful shoulder pads, the shirtband bow! *Russeks adv. in*
The Times.

I came down the sixth-floor corridor of the Arbogast Building, past the
World Wide Noodle Corporation, Zwinger & Rumsey, Accountants,
and the Ace Secretarial Service, Mimeographing Our Specialty. The

legend on the ground-glass panel next door said, 'Atlas Detective Agency, Noonan & Driscoll,' but Snapper Driscoll had retired two years before with a .38 slug between the shoulders, donated by a snow-bird in Tacoma, and I owned what good will the firm had. I let myself into the crummy ante-room we kept to impress clients, growled good morning at Birdie Claflin.

'Well, you certainly look like something the cat dragged in,' she said. She had a quick tongue. She also had eyes like dusty lapis lazuli, taffy hair, and a figure that did things to me. I kicked open the bottom drawer of her desk, let two inches of rye trickle down my craw, kissed Birdie square on her lush, red mouth, and set fire to a cigarette.

'I could go for you, sugar,' I said slowly. Her face was veiled, watch-ful. I stared at her ears, liking the way they were joined to her head. There was something complete about them; you knew they were there for keeps. When you're a private eye, you want things to stay put.

'Any customers?'

'A woman by the name of Sigrid Bjornsterne said she'd be back. A looker.'

'Swede?'

'She'd like you to think so.'

I nodded toward the inner office to indicate that I was going in there, and went in there. I lay down on the davenport, took off my shoes, and bought myself a shot from the bottle I kept underneath. Four minutes later, an ash-blonde with eyes the colour of unset opals, in a Nettie Rosenstein basic black dress and a baum-marten stole, burst in. Her bosom was heaving and it looked even better that way. With a gasp she circled the desk, hunting for some place to hide, and then, spotting the wardrobe where I keep a change of bourbon, ran into it. I got up and wandered out into the ante-room. Birdie was deep in a crossword puzzle.

'See anyone come in here?'

'Nope.' There was a thoughtful line between her brows, 'Say, what's a five-letter word meaning "trouble"?'

'Swede,' I told her, and went back inside. I waited the length of time it would take a small, not very bright, boy to recite *Ozymandias,* and, inching carefully along the wall, took a quick gander out the window. A thin galoot with stooping shoulders was being very busy reading a paper outside the Gristede store two blocks away. He hadn't been there an hour ago, but then, of course, neither had I. He wore a size seven dove-coloured hat from Browning King, a tan Wilson Brothers shirt

38

with pale-blue stripes, a J. Press foulard with a mixed red-and-white figure, dark-blue Interwoven socks, and an unshined pair of ox-blood London Character shoes. I let a cigarette burn down between my fingers until it made a small red mark, and then I opened the wardrobe.

'Hi,' the blonde said lazily. 'You Mike Noonan?' I made a noise that could have been 'Yes,' and waited. She yawned. I thought things over, decided to play it safe. I yawned. She yawned back, then, settling into a corner of the wardrobe, went to sleep. I let another cigarette burn down until it made a second red mark beside the first one, and then I woke her up. She sank into a chair, crossing a pair of gams that tightened my throat as I peered under the desk at them.

'Mr Noonan,' she said, 'you – you've got to help me.'

'My few friends call me Mike,' I said pleasantly.

'Mike.' She rolled the syllable on her tongue. 'I don't believe I've ever heard that name before. Irish?'

'Enough to know the difference between a gossoon and a bassoon.' . . .

S. J. PERELMAN

The Postman Visits Pam Ayres

Oh I woke up the other morning
    The sun was shining bright
The birds were singing in the trees
    And everything seemed all right.

Knock! Knock! I heard the Postman
    A-knocking at the door
Guess what he had for poor Pam Ayres?
    My little P44.

That's a form from the Inland Revenue
    In case you didn't know
'Cos if you earn a lot of money
    They'll come for you ho ho.

How shall I ever pay it all
    Now I'm a famous poet?
Well I'll do ads on the telly
    And as for the rest, I'll owe it.

So anyway that's life I think
    Plus VAT at 8%
Good heavens that's a lot of money
    And that's what I resent.

So I'll keep writing poems
    Just as they come up into my head
I'm famous now that I'm alive
    But what about when I'm dead?

PRIVATE EYE

Smiley All The Way To The Bank

The telephone rang by Le Carré's bed. He had been awake for hours, staring at the ceiling. He was washed up and he knew it. He hadn't had a new idea for years. He should never have left the Office.

It had been easy then. Scribbling away before breakfast. An hour snatched at the typewriter before some boring diplomatic reception. Five thousand words a week had seemed child's play in those days.

Who was ringing him? It could be Melvyn Barg, offering another interview on the South Bank Show. What was the point? He had nothing new to say.

He picked up the receiver.

'Yes?' he said, after a long pause.

So it was Hodder. It had been a long time. They had last met in Frankfurt. Staying together at the Hotel Weidenfeld. Murgatroyd had been there. He usually went over for the Book Fair.

'Le Carré,' said Hodder. 'We need you. There's a job. No one else can do it except you.'

Outside the rain beat a faint tattoo on the window pane. Le Carré picked his teeth abstractedly.

'You're talking to the wrong man,' he said. 'I'm finished with all that.'

His thoughts strayed to Cynthia. Why had she left him? Could it be because he was so boring? Or was she in love with Murgatroyd?

Hodder was speaking again. 'I've been talking it over with Stoughton.' He spoke excitedly. 'There's a train to Paddington at 3.15. We'll get a car to meet you. We count on you, John . . . .' . . .

The office hadn't changed much. The same handful of remaindered titles, gathering dust on the shelves. A gust of rain beat at the window, but Le Carré remained unaware of it.

The four men were sitting round a table. Hodder, looking a little greyer. Stoughton, thinning on top. And a young man Le Carré had never met before.

'Do you know Cohen?' Hodder enquired.

Le Carré mumbled a conventional greeting.

'Cohen will be handling your operation,' Hodder went on. 'It'll be a piece of cake.'

In the ashtray on the table was a pile of cigarette stubs. They looked as if they'd been there for a month. Le Carré was still wondering why the Old Firm wanted him back so badly.

The young man began to explain: 'Mr Le Carré,' he said, 'you remember the *Tinker, Tailor* affair?'

It had long been a legend in the firm. Le Carré's finest hour. A gust of wind ruffled the trees outside, as the spy-novelist's thoughts went back to the moment when had had first seen his name at the top of the best-seller lists. How unreal it all seemed now.

'Well, it's come up again,' Cohen went on. 'The BBC have bought it. It looks like the biggest thing since *Edward and Mrs Simpson*. They've even got Alec Guinness. It can't miss.'

So this is what they were leading up to, Le Carré thought. They want to cash in.

'We want to cash in,' said Hodder, 'it's as simple as that. You can do it in your sleep, old man. Just write anything that comes into your head – Russkies, Berlin Wall, all that sort of stuff. Absolutely down your street. Don't worry about plot, or anything complicated like that. Just get the words down, and we'll do the rest. We'll put your name big on the cover, print 100,000 in hardback and we'll all be ahead of the game again.'

'That's it,' said Stoughton. 'It's a winner. What do you say?'

Le Carré remained silent. His thoughts were already at work. An old Russian woman waiting for a bus in a Parisian street. A corpse on Hampstead Heath. A tie-up with the KGB. But where did Murgatroyd come in?

That was the real question . . . .

PRIVATE EYE

ANCIENT
AND
MODERN

Hymn

The Church's Restoration
  In eighteen-eighty-three
Has left for contemplation
  Not what there used to be.
How well the ancient woodwork
  Looks round the Rectr'y hall,
Memorial of the good work
  Of him who plann'd it all.

He who took down the pew-ends
  And sold them anywhere
But kindly spared a few ends
  Work'd up into a chair.
O worthy persecution
  Of dust! O hue divine!
O cheerful substitution,
  Thou varnishèd pitch-pine!

Church furnishing! Church furnishing!
  Sing art and crafty praise!
He gave the brass for burnishing,
  He gave the thick red baize,
He gave the new addition,
  Pull'd down the dull old aisle,
—To pave the sweet transition
  He gave th'encaustic tile.

Of marble brown and veinèd
  He did the pulpit make;
He order'd windows stainèd
  Light red and crimson lake.
Sing on, with hymns uproarious,
  Ye humble and aloof,
Look up! and oh how glorious
  He has restored the roof!

JOHN BETJEMAN

Prayer

O God. Let us give thanks for the warm embrace of the sun and the chaste kiss of the rain, thanking Thee as we match our splendid young limbs against each other in the rough and the tumble of our games together, so that at the last, rain-washed, sun-gilded, heaven-bent, we may repose upon Thine eternal changelessness and thus at the last when we are called to go whither we know not hence, we may see God and bask in the presence of His glory from henceforth unto henceforth. Amen . . . .

ALAN BENNETT
Forty Years On

The Prophet Melchizedek Foreseeth the Coming

And Lo, there shall come a day when there shall be no more trees. And on that day the cockatrice shall rejoice with the goat. And behold the ram shall lie down with the sheep and the leopard shall give suck to the porcupine. The little bee also shall dwell with the antelope and the lizard with the frog.

And on that day all my people shall praise the Lord.

PRIVATE EYE
Record: 'Private Eye Golden Satiricals'

From a Martyr's Journal

The fourth of May, in the year of our Lord, eighteen hundred and ninety-five, upon which day, exactly two years since, we began this our joyous crusade. Today the drums stopped beating. For the Lord, in his infinite wisdom, has seen fit to take Onwabi, Chief of the Sintu, unto Himself. And thus we stood, myself a child of God, and Owen, my faithful black helpmate in Christ, before the slowly advancing tribesmen. Naked they were, and devilishly painted, bearing nought before them save their pipes, from which would shoot at some unseen

46

command, their venomous darts. Unseen? Yea, to my eyes, but not so to Owen's. For as the first deadly dart sped towards my unprotected breast, that good soul threw himself before me, took the poisonous tip within his own heart, and dying fell. True friend, black body bleeding with blood as red as any fair-skinned Christian man's, how noble was thy sacrifice. And yet in vain! For following came the deluge. Dart after dart pierced my body. With every breath I breathed my breast heaved up a hundred quills. Dug deep with death and dying, yet lived I still.

JOHN HARDING AND JOHN BURROWS
The Golden Pathway Annual

Thought for the Day

It's awfully easy, isn't it, to forget the real, deep meaning of Christmas – the commercial meaning of Christmas. For many people it's simply a time of carols and church services and other rather sentimental celebrations. But for the tradesmen and manufacturers throughout the land such as myself it is a time when we have an opportunity to make a gigantic profit. It was our Lord I think himself who said, 'And there shall come a great profit throughout the land.' . . .

PRIVATE EYE
Record: 'Private Eye Golden Satiricals'

The Wassail of Figgy Duff
[Traditional]

> Oh Christmasse is i-cum
> Mark ye Robin's ruddy tum
> And ye winde itte bloweth very rough
> Rough rough
> Now do as ye be tolde
> To keepe us from ye colde
> And fille us up with Figgy, Figgy Duff
> Figgy Duff.

So merrily we sing,
For to make ye Welkin ring
Though of singing we have hadde quite enough
-Nough, -nough,
My maisters if you please
Give us a mouldy cheese
To eat with our Figgy, Figgy Duff
Figgy Duff.

If a cheese ye have not got
Then a groat must be our lot
As we dance round the Mistle Buff
Bough Buff!
If you haven't got a groat
You go and cut your throat
And ne'er have any Figgy, Figgy Duff
Figgy Duff.

MICHAEL FLANDERS

Take a Pew

The 11th verse of the 27th chapter of the book of the Genesis, 'But my brother Esau is an hairy man, but I am a smooth man' – 'But my brother Esau is an hairy man, but I am a smooth man.' Perhaps I can paraphrase this, say the same thing in a different way by quoting you some words from that grand old prophet, Nehemiah, Nehemiah 7-16:

And he said unto me, what seest thou
And I said unto him, lo

(Read next four lines twice)

I see the children of Bebai,
Numbering six hundred and seventy-three
And I see the children of Asgad
Numbering one thousand, four hundred and seventy-four.

48

There come times in the lives of each and every one of us when we turn aside from our fellows and seek the solitude and tranquillity of our own firesides. When we put up our feet and put on our slippers, and sit and stare into the fire. I wonder at such times whether your thoughts turn as mine do to those words I've just read you now.

They are very unique and very special words, words that express as so very few words do that sense of lack that lies at the very heart of modern existence. That I-don't-quite-know-what-it-is-but-I'm-not-getting-everything-out-of-life-that-I-should- be-getting sort of feeling. But they are more than this, these words, much much more – they are in a very real sense a challenge to each and every one of us here tonight. What is that challenge?

As I was on my way here tonight, I arrived at the station, and by an oversight I happened to come out by the way one is supposed to go in. And as I was coming out an employee of the railway company hailed me. 'Hey, Jack,' he shouted, 'where do you think you are going?' That at any rate was the gist of what he said. But, you know, I was grateful to him, because you see he put me in mind of the kind of question I felt I ought to be asking you here tonight. Where do you think you're going?

Very many years ago, when I was about as old as some of you are now, I went mountain climbing in Scotland with a very dear friend of mine. And there was this mountain, you see, and we decided to climb it. And so, very early one morning, we arose and began to climb. All day we climbed. Up and up and up. Higher and higher and higher. Till the valley lay very small below us, and the mists of the evening began to come down, and the sun to set. And when we reached the summit, we sat down to watch this most magnificent sight of the sun going down behind the mountain. And as we watched my friend very suddenly, and violently, vomited.

Some of us think life's a bit like that, don't we? But it isn't. You know life, life it's rather like opening a tin of sardines. We are all of us looking for the key. Some of us – some of us think we've found the key, don't we? We roll back the lid of the sardine tin of life, we reveal the sardines, the riches of life therein and we get them out, we enjoy them. But, you know, there's always a little bit in the corner you can't get out. I wonder – I wonder, is there a little bit in the corner of your life? I know there is in mine.

So now, as I draw to a close, I want you when you go out into the world, in times of trouble and sorrow and hopelessness and despair amid the hurly burly of modern life, if ever you're tempted to say, 'Oh stuff this for a lark!' I want you then to remember for comfort the words of my first text to you tonight . . . .

But my brother Esau is an hairy man, but I am a smooth man.

ALAN BENNETT
Beyond the Fringe

O Bloody Bloody Jesus

O bloody bloody Jesus
I love your blood so red
I love the bloody corpuscles
Streaming from your head

O bloody bloody Jesus
I love thy crimson tide
I love the bloody Roman spear
That got stuck in your side

O rare and bloody Jesus
I love thy hands that bled
I love the nails that pierced them
O Jesus red and dead

I'd love to drink the blood O Lord
That drips from off thy feet
And wash my hands and brush my teeth –
O Lord would that be sweet!

O bloody bloody Jesus
I love thy blood so red
I loved you when you were alive
I love you better dead.

TONY HENDRA AND SEAN KELLY
Not the Bible

Good Times Roll

[One of the Rutles Greatest Hits, a track from the album Sergeant Rutter's Darts Club Band]

Hour after hour
In an ivory tower
A thousand and nothings to do
Spending the day
In a colourful way
Blue upon blue upon blue
Psychadelicatessen.
   Fricassé chorus girls thigh
    Toffee and mackerel gâteau
    Pineapple pie in the sky
See how the good times roll
See how the good times roll
See how the good times roll away
Like ice in a drink
Invisible ink
Or dreams in the cold light of day
The children of rock and roll
Never grow old
They just fade away
Drifting along on
A cotton wool cloud
Dreaming of drum majorettes
Swastika nightingales
Croon tongue in cheek
An elephant never forgets
See how the good times roll
See how the good times roll
See how the good times roll away.

NEIL INNES

53

East River Rhapsody

The hooting of a tug boat
The honking of a horn,
The sweetest music
Wakes me every morn.
The clanging of a trash can
In the early morning dawn –
How lovely that cacophonous clash can be . . .
That's my East River Rhapsody.

Early morning,
Early morning.

Shalom, Mrs Kleinberg,
So tell me, what is new?

(MRS KLEINBERG *(spoken)*. Don't ask!)

Top o' the morning to you, Mrs Cassidy!
Would you be after cooking Irish Stew?

(MRS CASSIDY *(spoken)*. I got a great stew for you, Joey!)

Can you do my laundry
Quickly, Mister Wu?
Wanna wear a clean shirt
Saturday for Sue!
Buon Giorno, Rocco baby,
For a dime-a- shine-a my shoe!
How's your mamma? How's your poppa?
What's the world a-doing to you?

No music takes me higher
Than the music of Lower East Side

The siren of a squad car
Which comes and goes along,
A dimly heard Salvation Army song
A baby who's a shouter,
The schoolyard going strong,
The wind will take my melody out to sea . . .
That's my East River
My East River Rhapsody!

JULIAN MORE
Songbook

54

I Hold Your Hand in Mine

I hold your hand in mine, dear,
I press it to my lips.
I take a healthy bite from
Your dainty finger tips.

My joy would be complete, dear,
If you were only here,
But still I keep your hand as
A precious souvenir.

The night you died I cut it off,
I really don't know why.
For now each time I kiss it, I
Get bloodstains on my tie.

I'm sorry now I killed you, for
Our love was something fine,
And till they come to get me, I
Shall hold your hand in mine.

TOM LEHRER

April in Wisconsin

When it's April in Wisconsin,
And I'm sitting here in Rome,
I am longin' for Wisconsin
And my huckleberry home.
Are young meadowlarks still singin'?
Is the sky the same old blue?
When it's April in Wisconsin,
And young lovers' hearts are dancin'
What's become of you?
Do you miss me?
Is there someone else you've found?
Now it's springtime,
Yes it's springtime
With new lovers

Around
But I pray that you're still waitin'
And I'll hear from you today.
When it's April in Wisconsin
And you're lookin' so entrancin'
Four thousand miles away.

JULIAN MORE
Songbook

Noël, Noël

Intro:
Dear Whomever It May Concern at the BBC,
Pass this letter to the Brains Trust very urgently.

Verse 1
    Throughout the war we soldiered on
    When almost every hope had gone
    And pinned our flagging faith to Vera Lynn.
    We turned out railings into tanks
    And smiled politely at the Yanks
    When all they sent across was Errol Flynn.
But when the lights went on we saw the vict'ry was a sham,
The Lion's share turned out to be a smaller slice of Spam.
    The bluebirds came one dreary day,
    Looked at Dover and flew away
    And grim spectators murmured, 'Why can't I?'
    They might go down to the sea in ships
    But that's forbidden by Stafford Cripps
And the nightingale in Berkeley Square can only sit and cry.

Chorus
So – could you please inform us who it was that won the war?
The outcome isn't certain, Heaven knows.
Now everyone's so keen to put the Germans on their feet,
For apparently
The majority
Are really rather sweet.

Meanwhile back in Britain we're still lining up in rows
To buy enough to keep ourselves alive.
So could you please inform us how we came to lose the war
That we won in nineteen-forty-five?

Verse 2

Our former wealth is going to
Augment the Inland Revenue
And though our situation might seem hard
At least you needn't work these days,
The Ministry of Labour pays
You well, provided someone's stamped your card.
The National Health is failing fast and no one gives a fig,
The Corpses will look delightful in a newly-issued wig.
Our image for posterity
Is one of grim austerity,
The Socialist Nirvana's on the way:
New ministries proliferate
Whose function is to allocate
To everyone his fair and proper share of sweet FA.

Chorus 2

So – could you please inform us how we came to lose the peace?
Perhaps it's best to be the losing side,
Now that the Americans are sponsoring the Japs,
Taking the view
That but for a few
They're awfully decent chaps.
Such a strange development is wounding to our pride,
The countrymen of Wellington and Clive,
So Bevin only knows how Britain came to lose the peace
When she won in nineteen-forty-five,
Four, three, two, one,
Yes *won* in nineteen-forty-five?

PETER NICHOLS
Privates on Parade

Read

Letters

A Poor Correspondent

Dear Joyce,

Just a line 'in haste' to apologise for not writing before, so excuse the scrawl. Keep promising myself I'll sit down and write you a really good long letter one of these days, but never seem to get the chance. You're such a good letter-writer it makes me feel ashamed of my own poor efforts. I suppose it's the way you 'put' things. I always feel 'I wish I'd thought of that' – but then you've got the gift, haven't you? When I sit down to write it all flies out of my head. But one of these days I really will sit down and write you a good long letter.

Well, sorrry to have 'gone on' so long – I never 'know when to stop,' that's my trouble. Must rush to catch post, so I'm afraid I'll have to close.

> All my love,
> Eileen

PS. Knew there was something I meant to say – everyone is well and sends their love.

> MICHAEL FRAYN
> *The Mails Must Go Through*

Letter to Not Yet The Times

DEDUCTION

From Mr Marmaduke Garter

Sir,
Surely the answer to odd socks is odd feet?
   I am,

> Yours faithfully,
> MARMADUKE GARTER
> Bypass Rd,
> Rotherham,
> Yorks.

> NOT YET THE TIMES

Dear Mr Dickens

Dear Mr Dickens,

Six months of silence since we dispatched our manuscripts to you! Only the cry of the curlew, the wind on the heath and the solicitor's letter forbidding my brother Branwell from writing to you again, to ease our solitude!

Did the crate of MSS perhaps not reach you? No matter; it is God's will. The hard frost and the keen wind have done nothing for my sisters' constitution; but if they are spared, they shall each write at least one more novel before they are called to eternity. My sister Emily begs me to inquire what your opinion is of the title 'Withering Heights'.

Forgive me, Master, if I adopt the course of writing to you again. Day and night I find neither rest nor peace. If I sleep I am disturbed by tormenting dreams in which I see *you*. How can I endure life if I make no effort to ease its sufferings? You showed me a *little* interest, when you advised me to write to the *Leeds Intelligencer,* now I need the continuance of that interest as I need bread. The winter has been bitterly cold; life at Haworth wears away; one day resembles another. I hope, I pine, for a letter from you; day follows day and no letter comes, unless a missive from you was among the batch my brother sold to a bookseller in Bradford, to pay for medicine.

Perhaps you received our manuscripts but cannot read our handwriting. As soon as I shall have saved enough money to go to London I shall go there, and visit you, and read you our works from the beginning to the end. If you have compassion, you will not turn me away. I need very little affection from those I love.

Yours respectfully,
Charlotte Brontë

KEITH WATERHOUSE
Letters Tied With Blue

You Write . . .

Dear Emma Jane,

My wife and I are avid watchers of television. Being ordinary folk leading sad, humdrum lives, we particularly appreciate programmes that bring celebrities and personalities into our humble living-room. I wonder whether you've ever noticed the extraordinary resemblance between Jimmy Hill and Katie Boyle? I think they must be related, but my wife Dorothy doesn't agree. Could you settle this argument once and for all?

> Yours sincerely,
> D. Tupp (Mr)
> Streatham

Dear Emma Jane,

I need your advice. My husband and I are an ordinary couple who have been happily married for nine years. Recently, however he has taken to reading *Men Only* and *Curious,* entering *The Sun's* 'Guilty Pleasures' competition, sticking the same paper's saucy Page 3 lovelies on the wall of his do-it-yourself room, neglecting his whippet, ignoring his homework, letting the Black and Decker drill I bought him for Christmas lie idle and coming home as late as 6.30 on a Friday night. He says he still loves me, that I am flesh and blood, whereas the shameless magazine girls are mere harmless shadows, but I'm afraid he's become a victim of the permissive society. What can I do?

> Yours sincerrely,
> Ethel Putts
> Ealing

> WILLIAM DONALDSON
> *Letters to Emma Jane*

63

Official Letter

I beg to advise you of the following facts of which I happened to be the equally impartial and horrified witness.

Today, at roughly twelve noon, I was present on the platform of a bus which was proceeding up the rue de Courcelles in the direction of the Place Champerret. The aforementioned bus was fully laden – more than fully laden, I might even venture to say, since the conductor had accepted an overload of several candidates, without valid reason and actuated by an exaggerated kindness of heart which caused him to exceed the regulations and which, consequently, bordered on indulgence. At each stopping place the perambulations of the outgoing and incoming passengers did not fail to provoke a certain disturbance which incited one of these passengers to protest, though not without timidity. I should mention that he went and sat down as and when this eventuality became possible.

I will append to this short account this addendum: I had occasion to observe this passenger some time subsequently in the company of an individual whom I was unable to identify. The conversation which they were exchanging with some animation seemed to have a bearing on questions of an aesthetic nature.

In view of these circumstances, I would request you to be so kind, Sir, as to intimate to me the inference which I should draw from these facts and the attitude which you would then deem appropriate that I adopt in re the conduct of my subsequent mode of life.

Anticipating the favour of your reply, believe me to be, Sir, your very obedient servant at least.

RAYMOND QUENEAU (Tr. BARBARA WRIGHT)
Exercises in Style

Letter to the San Serriffe Times

From Vice-Admiral the Venerable the Deputy Keeper of the Musket, QC.

Sir,

On February 27, 1964, you were kind enough to publish a letter above the subscription below. I hope you will now be so good as to repeat that courtesy.

   I have the honour to remain,

> Yours faithfully,
> DOUGLAS FERGUSON
> The Deputy Keeper's Lodge
> Bodoni

> GEOFFREY TAYLOR
> *The Guardian 1 April 1978*

Yours Faithfully

Sir,

Every time an ice-cream van approaches this village with its dulcimers blaring, more molehills appear on our once beautiful lawn. It is the same everywhere in this district, and many of us believe the noise in some way excites the animals. I wrote to our MP to see what could be done about this nuisance, but no action was forthcoming. Moreover, my husband now finds it impossible to buy muffins anywhere. We have voted Conservative for many years, but now we are beginning to wonder.

> Yours faithfully,
> Sylvia Cront
> Ramblings
> Quantum Posset
> Dorset

> PAUL JENNINGS
> *I Must Have Imagined It*

THEATRES

of

THE

ABSURD

Setting the Scene

The phone rings. MRS DRUDGE *seems to have been waiting for it to do so and for the last few seconds has been dusting it with an intense concentration. She snatches it up.*

MRS DRUDGE *(into phone).* Hello, the drawing-room of Lady Muldoon's country residence one morning in early spring? . . . Hello! – the draw — Who? Who did you wish to speak to? I'm afraid there is no one of that name here, this is all very mysterious and I'm sure it's leading up to something, I hope nothing is amiss for we, that is Lady Muldoon and her houseguests, are here cut off from the world, including Magnus, the wheelchair-ridden half-brother of her ladyship's husband Lord Albert Muldoon who, ten years ago, went out for a walk on the cliffs and was never seen again – and all alone, for they had no children . . . .
Should a stranger enter our midst, which I very much doubt, I will tell him you called. Good-bye.

She puts down the phone and catches sight of the previously seen suspicious character who has now entered again, more suspiciously than ever, through the french windows. He senses her stare, freezes, and straightens up.

SIMON. Ah! – hello there! I'm Simon Gascoyne, I hope you don't mind, the door was open so I wandered in. I'm a friend of Lady Muldoon, the lady of the house, having made her acquaintance through a mutual friend, Felicity Cunningham, shortly after moving into this neighbourhood just the other day.

MRS DRUDGE. I'm Mrs Drudge. I don't live in but I pop in on my bicycle when the weather allows to help in the running of charming though somewhat isolated Muldoon Manor. Judging by the time *(she glances at the clock)* you did well to get here before high water cut us off for all practical purposes from the outside world.

SIMON. I took the short cut over the cliffs and followed one of the old smugglers' paths through the treacherous swamps that surround this strangely inaccessible house.

MRS DRUDGE. Yes, many visitors have remarked on the topographical quirk in the local strata whereby there are no roads leading from the Manor, though there *are* ways of getting *to* it, weather allowing.

SIMON. Yes, well I must say it's a lovely day so far.

MRS DRUDGE. Ah, but now that the cuckoo-beard is in bud there'll be fog before the sun hits Foster's Ridge.

SIMON. I say, it's wonderful how you country people really know weather.

MRS DRUDGE *(suspiciously)*. Know whether what?

SIMON *(glancing out of the window)*. Yes, it does seem to be coming on a bit foggy.

MRS DRUDGE. The fog is very treacherous around here – it rolls off the sea without warning, shrouding the cliffs in a deadly mantle of blind man's buff.

SIMON. Yes, I've heard it said.

MRS DRUDGE. I've known whole week-ends when Muldoon Manor, as this lovely old Queen Anne house is called, might as well have been floating on the pack ice for all the good it would have done phoning the police. It was on such a week-end as this that Lord Muldoon who had lately brought his beautiful bride back to the home of his ancestors, walked out of this house ten years ago, and his body was never found. . . .

TOM STOPPARD
The Real Inspector Hound

Fragment of a Greek Tragedy

CHORUS. O suitably-attired-in-leather-boots
Head of a traveller, wherefore seeking whom
Whence by what way how purposed art thou come
To this well-nightingaled vicinity?
My object in inquiring is to know.
But if you happen to be deaf and dumb
And do not understand a word I say,
Then wave your hand, to signify as much.

ALC. I journeyed hither a Boetian road.

CHORUS. Sailing on horseback, or with feet for oars?

ALC. Plying with speed my partnership of legs.

CHORUS. Beneath a shining or a rainy Zeus?

ALC. Mud's sister, not himself, adorns my shoes.

CHORUS. To learn your name would not displease me much.

ALC. Not all that men desire do they obtain.

CHORUS. Might I then hear at what your presence shoots?

ALC. A Shepherd's questioned mouth informed me that —

CHORUS. What? for I know not yet what you will say.

ALC. Nor will you ever, if you interrupt.

CHORUS. Proceed , and I will hold my speechless tongue.

ALC. This house was Eriphyla's, no one's else.

CHORUS. Nor did he shame his throat with shameful lies.

ALC. May I then enter, passing through the door?

CHORUS. Go chase into the house a lucky foot.
　　And, O my son, be, on the one hand, good,
　　And do not, on the other hand, be bad;
　　For that is very much the safest plan.

ALC. I go into the house with heels and speed.

CHORUS.

Strophe
In speculation
I would not willingly acquire a name
　　For ill-digested thought;
　　But after pondering much
To this conclusion I at last have come:
　　Life is uncertain.
　　This truth I have written deep
　　In my reflective midriff

71

On tablets not of wax,
Nor with a pen did I inscribe it there,
For many reasons. *Life,* I say, *is not*
    A stranger to uncertainty.
Not from the flight of omen-yelling fowls
    This fact did I discover,
Nor did the Delphine tripod bark it out,
    Nor yet Dodona.
Its native ingenuity sufficed
    My self-taught diaphragm.

Antistrophe
    Why should I mention
The Inachean daughter, loved of Zeus?
    Her whom of old the gods,
    More provident than kind,
Provided with four hoofs, two horns, one tail,
    A gift not asked for,
    And sent her forth to learn
    The unfamiliar science
    Of how to chew the cud.
She therefore, all about the Argive fields,
Went cropping pale green grass and nettle-tops,
    Nor did they disagree with her.
But yet, howe'er nutritious, such repasts
    I do not hanker after:
Never may Cypris for her seat select
    My dappled liver!
Why should I mention Io? Why indeed?
    I have no notion why.

Epode
But now does my boding heart,
Unhired, unaccompanied, sing
A strain not meet for the dance
Yea even the palace appears
To my yoke of circular eyes
(The right, nor omit I the left)

Like a slaughterhouse, so to speak,
Garnished with woolly deaths
And many shipwrecks of cows.
I therefore in a Cissian strain lament;
And to the rapid
Loud, linen-tattering thumps upon my chest
Resounds in concert
The battering of my unlucky head.

ERI *(within)*. O, I am smitten with a hatchet's jaw;
And that in deed and not in word alone.

CHORUS. I thought I heard a sound within the house
Unlike the voice of one that jumps for joy.

ERI. He splits my skull, not in a friendly way,
Once more: he purposes to kill me dead.

CHORUS. I would not be reputed rash, but yet
I doubt if all be gay within the house.

ERI. O! O! another stroke! that makes the third.
He stabs me to the heart against my wish.

CHORUS. If that be so, thy state of health is poor;
But thine arithmetic is quite correct.

A. E. HOUSMAN

A Tub Called Tractatus
[after Tom Stoppard]

INSPECTOR LEADWIG. I have reason to believe there is a tortoise in
one of your ice cream tubs.

FILBERT RILE. That is a matter that can wait. There's no ghost in the
tub, not even a disposition. What of the tongueless tea-taster with a
bullet in his heart and a Masonic apron on his crotch?

LEADWIG. If we solve one we solve the other: show the tortoise the
way out of the tub and the difficulty will melt away.

73

Outside in pelting rain a one-armed bandit hops by clutching a stuffed giraffe.

RILE. I don't see —

LEADWIG. Ha! *(he yanks a tortoise out of the tub called Tractatus.)* Now if it had been hibernating in the Leibniz surprise it would have been a different matter.

RILE. But what of the identity of the murderer?

LEADWIG. Of what we cannot speak, thereof we must be silent . . . .

RILE. That is a category of a different colour. Say no more. I am as patriotic as the next man.

The tubs stand to attention as the curtain falls to the national anthem.

T. GRIFFITHS

Savonarola Brown
[*after Shakespeare*]

Time. Afternoon of same day.

Scene Lucrezia's Laboratory. Retorts, test-tubes, etc. On small Renaissance table, up centre, is a great poison-bowl, the contents of which are being stirred by the FIRST APPRENTICE. *The* SECOND APPRENTICE *stands by, watching him.*

SECOND APPRENTICE.
For whom is the brew destin'd?

FIRST APPRENTICE.

                    I know not.
Lady Lucrezia did but lay on me
Injunctions as regards the making of 't,
The which I have obey'd. It is compounded
Of a malignant and a deadly weed
Found not save in the Gulf of Spezia,

And one small phial of 't, I am advis'd,
Were more than 'nough to slay a regiment
Of Messer Malatesta's condottieri
In all their armour.

SECOND APPRENTICE.
                I can well believe it
Mark how the purple bubbles froth upon
The evil surface of its nether slime!

Enter LUCREZIA.

LUCREZIA (*To* FIRST APPRENTICE).
Is't done, Sir Sluggard?

FIRST APPRENTICE.
                Madam, to a turn.

LUCREZIA.
Had it not been so, I with mine own hand
Would have outpour'd it down thy gullet, knave.
See, here's a ring of cunningly-wrought gold
That I, on a dark night, did purchase from
A goldsmith on the Ponte Vecchio.
Small was his shop, and hoar of visage he.
I did bemark that from the ceiling's beams
Spiders had spun their webs for many a year,
The which hung erst like swathes of gossamer
Seen in the shadows of a fairy glade,
But now most woefully were weighted o'er
With gather'd dust. Look well now at the ring!
Touch'd here, behold, it opes a cavity
Capacious of three drops of yon fell stuff.
Dost heed? Whoso then puts it on his finger
Dies, and his soul is from his body rapt
To Hell or Heaven as the case may be.
Take thou this toy and pour the three drops in.

Hands ring to FIRST APPRENTICE *and comes down centre.*

So, Sav'narola, thou shalt learn that I
Utter no threats but I do make them good.
Ere this day's sun hath wester'd from the view
Thou art to preach from out the Loggia
Dei Lanzi to the cits in the Piazza.
I, thy Lucrezia, will be upon the steps
To offer thee with phrases seeming-fair
That which shall seal thine eloquence for ever.
O mighty lips that held the world in spell
But would not meet these little lips of mine
In the sweet way that lovers use – O thin,
Cold, tight-drawn, bloodless lips, which natheless I
Deem of all lips the most magnifical
In this our city –

Enter the Borgias' FOOL .

        Well, Fool, what's thy latest?

FOOL.
Aristotle's or Zeno's, Lady—'tis neither latest nor last. For, marry, if
the cobbler stuck to his last, then were his latest his last *in rebus
ambulantibus*. Argal, I stick at nothing but cobble-stones, which, by the
same token, are stuck to the road by men's fingers.

LUCREZIA.
How many crows may nest in a grocer's jerkin?

FOOL.
A full dozen at cock-crow, and something less under the dog-star, by
reason of the dew, which lies heavy on men taken by the scurvy.

LUCREZIA (*to* FIRST APPRENTICE).
Methinks the Fool is a fool.

FOOL.
And therefore, by auricular deduction, am I own twin to the Lady
Lucrezia!

Sings:

When pears hang green on the garden wall
  With a nid, and a nod, and a niddy-niddy-o

Then prank you, lads and lasses all
    With a yea and a nay and a niddy-o.

But when the thrush flies out o' the frost
    With a nid, (*etc.*)
'Tis time for loons to count the cost,
    With a yea (*etc.*)

Enter the PORTER .

PORTER.
O my dear Mistress, there is one below
Demanding to have instant word of thee.
I told him that your Ladyship was not
At home. Vain perjury! He would not take
Nay for an answer.

LUCREZIA.
Ah? What manner of man
Is he?

PORTER.
          A personage the like of whom
Is wholly unfamiliar to my gaze
Cowl'd is he, but I saw his great eyes glare
From their deep sockets in such wise as leopards
Glare from their caverns, crouching ere they spring
On their reluctant prey.

LUCREZIA.
              And what name gave he?

PORTER (*after a pause*).
Something-arola.

LUCREZIA.
    Savon? (PORTER *nods.*) Show him up.

Exit PORTER . . .

MAX BEERBOHM

from *Evening Dress Essential*
[*a little known T. S. Eliot play*]

CEDRIC. Shadows outpace us. These, Lydia, are dark times
    We live in.

LYDIA. Dark, Cedric,
    Dark. The world turns on its axis
    Darkly.

CEDRIC. Even as we speak
    The worm is at his business in the bud.

LYDIA. Busy devourer! Taking tea this morning –
    You know my passion for Darjeeling, dear –
    I thought I caught the sound of rattling bones.

CEDRIC (*impulsively*). I heard them too! Battling through the crowd
    At Fortnum's, for my special foie gras,
    I caught their rattle.

LYDIA (*bitterly*). A battle? For a rattle?
    Grim jest! (*Starts.*) Oh, do I hear them still?

CEDRIC/LYDIA. Darkly,
    We listen

CEDRIC (*after a pause, gloomily*). Lydia, Lydia,
    I have heard their sound, their rattle,
    In the dread desert wastes.
    In the dread desert wastes
    (Over a cocktail after coitus)
    Those bones echoed around me.

LYDIA (*mysteriously*). Cedric, Cedric,
    At this violet hour,
    I can hear
    Their echo.

CEDRIC. In Africa last spring –
  While on a mission for the Foreign Office –
  I forgot the squeaking of pens, the taping of Reds,
  And paid a visit to a lazaretto.
  The lepers' sores
  Blaze for me yet in Hampstead.
  Yes, Lydia, they burn.

LYDIA. Cedric, Cedric,
  I can feel
  That heat.

CEDRIC (*casually, lighting a cigarette*). Please, Lydia,
  Do not upset yourself. Look on the bright
  Side. Yesterday, wasn't it, your shares
  Rose on the Stock Exchange?
  I shall ring for drinks.
  A gin and tonic, is it? . . .

PAUL BAILEY
Peter Smart's Confession

Perseverance

or Half a Coronet
An Operetta In the Gilbertian Manner

Scene. The Terrace of the House of Commons – looking from the windows of the House, i.e. towards the river. The audience sees at the back the parapet of the river-wall, and behind them are the sails of fishing-vessels which, for reasons unknown, are made fast to the wall.

  Discovered, PERSEVERANCE *and* LUCY *, with chorus of fifty* FISHER-GIRLS *in bright-coloured dresses and black woollen stockings. They carry baskets of fish suspended from their shoulders by pink ribbons, and do absurd little movements with admirable uniformity.*

PERSEVERANCE *and* LUCY, *with* CHORUS OF FISHER-GIRLS .

Fifty fisher-girls are we
Selling fishes from the sea,
Suiting our ways to our wares:
Fifty fisher-girls or more,
As we think we said before,
Suiting our ways to our wares,
    Though nobody cares:
Each fish in the ocean
We fit with a motion—
With old-fashioned grace
We offer you plaice;

For haddock or cod
We've a coy little nod,
And a virginal pose
For sole or soft roes:
Your fancy exciting
With winkles and whiting,
Although it's not clear
Why we're selling fish here,

Fifty-fish — fifty fish —
Fifty-fish — fifty fish —
Fifty-fish — fifty pretty fisher-girls are we.

Enter, arm in arm, RUDOLF *and* ROBERT, *who, between them, for reasons which will appear, hold the title of Viscount Bunion. They are in court dress.*
    RUDOLF *has a very high and fruity tenor voice, and speaks his dialogue as if he has a large potato in his throat and may burst into song at any moment.* ROBERT'*s voice is more normal, and even gruff. He is a baritone or bass. They are twins, but need not be strikingly alike.*
    The FISHER-GIRLS, *head by* PERSEVERANCE, *greet the twins.*

PERSEVERANCE. Lord Rudolf! Will you purchase a plaice?

LUCY. Lord Robert, may I sell you a sole?

RUDOLF (*brushing them aside*). Pray observe the decencies of etiquette, young ladies. There is no Lord Rudolf—

ROBERT (*gloomily*). Lord Robert does not exist.

RUDOLF. There is only the Viscount Bunion.

PERSEVERANCE. Yes, but which is he?

RUDOLF AND ROBERT (*linking arms again and striking an attitude*). *We* are the Viscount Bunion.

LUCY. What, both of you? . . .

PERSEVERANCE (*very arch – playing to* ROBERT *and* RUDOLF *alternately*).

> Though I am loath
> To plight my troth
> With exact particularity,
>   Yet I might part
>   With hand and heart
> On terms of honest parity:
>   I will not kiss
>   The one – like this –   (*does so*)
>   Unless I kiss the other: (*does so*)
>   Pray hold my hand,   (RUDOLF *takes it*)
>   But understand
> You share it with your brother.
>   (ROBERT *takes it too*)

CHORUS.

> Arrangement unromantical!
> With equity pedantical
>   She will not kiss
>   The one (like this)   (*all kiss everybody*)
> Unless she hugs the other.
> This proposition frantical
> Is almost transatlantical
>   – antical:
> Half a loaf is not much fun,
> But half a lady's worse than none.

PERSEVERANCE.

> On Monday night
>   I'm your delight   (*to* RUDOLF)
> (But, of course, with due propriety);
>   On Tuesday (noon)
>   I change my tune

And bask in *your* society: (*to* ROBERT)
  So neither swain
  Can well complain
That he is hardly treated,
  For if I do
  The same for two,
Which is the one that's cheated?

CHORUS.   Engagement mathematical!
                  With equity fanatical
                    She means to do
                    The same for two;
                  So neither one is cheated.
                  One must not be dogmatical,
                  But we are still emphatical
                                    – phatical
                  Half a loaf is *quantum suff.*
                  But half a lady's not enough.

CHORUS.   Here comes an old maid!
                    Ha, ha! What a joke!
                  She's as plain as a spade,
                    And as tough as an oak.
                  The suitors have tarried,
                  Her plans have miscarried,
                  She'll never be married.
                    Ha, ha! What a joke!

                  Here comes an old maid!
                  She's extremely decayed,
                  Her face is mislaid,
                  She's frowsy and frayed,
                  She's a sight in the shade.
                    Ha, ha!
                  So with chivalrous feelings we bawl
                  'She'll never be married at all!'
                    There's one thing ag'inst her,

She's made for a spinster,
But no one's convinced her –
Ha, ha! What a joke!

Enter the LADY CHANCELLOR *– a tremendously tall contralto, in her robes of office, with full-bottomed wig. Either she or an attendant should carry the Great Seal.*

THE LADY CHANCELLOR (*recitative*).
        I am the Lady Chancellor, I am,
        But once I was a nurse and drove a pram.
                (*Song*)
        Two lovely twins they trusted to my care,
        Alike in size, in feature, form and hair.
        No marks. No moles. But *I* knew which was what,
        For one was musical – the other not.

CHORUS.   Ah, one was musical – the other not!

THE LADY CHANCELLOR.
        The elder babe would crow and croon all day,
        And cried for 'Momma' in the key of A:
        The other seldom sang, and, if he did,
        Was out of tune. Ah, how I loved that kid!

CHORUS.   Though out of tune, she dearly loved that kid.

THE LADY CHANCELLOR.
        What if my age is rather more than middle?
        For his sweet sake I now resolve the riddle.
        If one can sing—the rightful Earl is he: (*pointing at twins*)
        The other, still more blest, shall marry ME. . . .

                    FINALE

RUDOLF.   Take a dainty paradox,
        Dress it like a chocolate-box –
        Take two babies – mix them well:
        Take one spinster – give her H—!

Take some logic – chop it thin;
Take some tunes and rub them in:
One patter-song, and don't forget
Your unaccompanied quartet:
Take a little love, but – hush!
Not enough to raise a blush.
By degrees you'll find you'll get a
Rather popular operetta—

CHORUS.   Loved by curate, Kew and Quetta – (*ad lib*)
And it is a tip-top property –
Yes, there is no properer property
    Than a jocular
    Never shockular
        Proper, popular, popular, operette.

A. P. HERBERT

The Absurdity of Being Dundown

GERALD GROSVENOR *enters in a scarlet military tunic, carrying a pith helmet with plumes.*

GERALD. Good morning, Aunt Sedilia.

LADY DUNDOWN. The weather is immaterial. Gerald, do I detect a somewhat military note in your appearance? What is the reason for these warlike habilaments?

GERALD. I have been called to the Colours.

LADY DUNDOWN. Indeed? Whereabouts?

GERALD. South Africa.

LADY DUNDOWN. South Africa? I trust that will not interfere with your attendance at my dances?

GERALD. I'm afraid so.

LADY DUNDOWN. Tsk, tsk. How can the Zulu expect to be treated as civilised people when they declare war in the middle of the season!

GERALD. It's not the Zulu, Aunt Sedilia. It's the Boer.

LADY DUNDOWN. It comes to the same thing. I have never understood this liking for war. It panders to instincts already catered for within the scope of any respectable domestic establishment. Which brings me to my point. Your marriage. I have been going through my list and have hit upon the ideal person. Lady Maltby.

GERALD. Lady Maltby!

LADY DUNDOWN. Constance Maltby. (*She rises from wheelchair.*) I can walk. It's just that I'm so rich I don't need to. Consider her advantages. She is in full possession of all her faculties, plus the usual complement of limbs . . . and enough in such matters, I always think, is as good as a feast.

GERALD. I have heard it said that her legs leave something to be desired.

LADY DUNDOWN. All legs leave *something* to be desired, do they not? That is part of their function and all of their charm. But to continue. Like all stout women she is very fat, but then, it would be inconsistent of her to be otherwise, would it not?

GERALD. Is she not connected with Trade?

LADY DUNDOWN. Trade? Nonsense. Her father made a fortune by introducing the corset to the Esquimaux. That is not trade. It is philanthropy.

GERALD. And she is very old fashioned besides.

LADY DUNDOWN. If by that you mean she dresses like her mother, yes she is. But then all women dress like their mothers, that is their tragedy. No man ever does. That is his. You have something to say?

GERALD. Yes, Aunt Sedilia. You see, I have been engaged before. Several times.

LADY DUNDOWN. I am aware that you have been engaged, though, if I may say so, much after the manner of a public lavatory . . . often and for very short periods . . .

ALAN BENNETT
Forty Years On

Cambridge Footbrakes
Some sketches not used in last year's show, performed by those of last year's cast not snapped up by the BBC. 'Hilarious' *St Mark's Cathedral Annexe, Ratbone Place.*

Doncaster Polytechnic Drama Group
Shakespeare's *Midnight Summer's Dream,* in an unusual Caribbean setting which brings out the neo-colonialist undertow of the Bard's writing. Full reggae score by Doncaster Natty Dread Jug Blowers. *Masonic Lodge, Wilkiehall Street.*

The Perforated Umbrella Tricycle Group
'The 1967 Eurovision Song Contest.' A retelling of the Brontë sisters' story in modern dress, and introducing hitherto unknown Brontë sister Tracey. 'The audience chuckled a bit'— *Scotsman. Longniddry Town Hall. (76 bus out of Edinburgh through Musselburgh, then walk.)*

University of Dodge City, USA, Mime Group
A silent reading of poems by East German protest poet Wolfgang Backhaus, using masks, mime, dance, scenery, curtains, stage, chairs and a glass of water. *St Mary's Church Hall, Glasgow. (Fast, regular trains from Edinburgh.)*

The Cambridge Lights
And now for something completely offal! A load of tripe performed by a bunch of faggots! 'Last year's off-cuts' — *Scotsman. Butcher's Hall, Grindlay Street.*

Macrepertory Company
'Twa's Company. Three's Nane.' All-Scottish one-man show. Based on Brecht's best remarks. *The Cellar, St Mungo's Bus Shelter.* (13, 17, 45, 64 and 187.)

Gay Sweatshirt Drama Group
'Terence and Emlyn.' A searching examination of the tempestuous relationship between these two if they had ever happened to meet. *The Cottage, Heriot-Watt Street.*

Harwich Customs and Excise Drama Group
'Missing. Believed at Orly'. A merciless, searching, hilarious, tragi-comic, Brechtian, powerful, bawdy, inglorious examination of the international luggage-losing system, translated from the Polish of Wojtyla. *Departure Lounge, Waverley Station.*

New York All Night Bus Queue Drama Group
A troupe of players formed during an enforced meeting one night at New York's central bus station, this is their improvisation based on an all-night vigil by a group of passengers stranded in a New York coach depot. 'Makes *A Chorus Line* look easy.' *St Grindlay's Kiosk, Haymarket.*

Albanian People's Mime Group
A polished and fast-moving exhibition of water colours. Coffee. *Vestry, St Mary's Cathedral.*

Exeter Street Wanderers
An authentic Japanese Noh puppet 'n' mime version of Lady Hamilton's tax difficulties after Lord Nelson's death, from the East German of Krimpel. *Masonic Cocktail Bar, North Bristol Hotel.*

North British Hotel Waiters Theatre Group
'Supergratuity!' A scathing science fiction musical exposing the malpractices of interplanetary catering, showing how cheap immigrant Martian kitchen labour is ripped off on a galactic, almost Brechtian scale. 'The *soupe du jour* space disaster is almost unbearably moving' – *Scotsman.*

The Canine Battersea Amateur Dramatic Company
All-dog cast in a new version of 'Rover's Return', the only play written by Weill without Brecht. *Leith Dog Kennels.*

The Open University Archery Society
'The Assassination of the Ex-Shah of Iran, as Performed by the Inmates of the Open University Archery Society.' A sober yet powerful examination of the different ways in which the OUAS could plug His Serene Highness and get the big prize offered by Iran. 'I was transfixed' – *Scotsman. Craigmillar Castle grounds.*

87

The Cambridge Footpads

This revue will 'knock you out'! Every joke has a 'kick'! Good old-fashioned 'knockabout' humour from a team of expert 'muggers'! *St Mungo Cathedral, Top Corner, Left-hand Aisle.*

The Morningside Old Ladies Appreciation Society

Group of elderly Edinburgh citizens who appear in a different hall every day, in the audience, conducting a subdued yet puzzled discussion on Brecht.

Cooperative de Fruites et Legumes de Bretagne

Twice daily performance in which Breton amateur farmers angrily block the aisles and stage with tractors in a protest against the untimely death of Bertolt Brecht. *Scottish Dairies Recreation Hall, Dalkeith.*

PUNCH

Some House-party Maugham

Up stage left at the writing desk, young Freddie Manningtree begins to write a letter, then tears it in two and throws the pieces on to the desk. Begins a second letter, this time rolls it into a ball and throws it on the floor. Begins third letter, then unrolls second letter, and pieces together the first, compares all three. Finally rejects all three. Sits facing light pouring in through French window — man in attitude of dejection. Takes cigarette case and matches from dressing-gown pockets, lights a cigarette. Mother's voice from garden, 'Getting along all right, Freddie?' [Some laughter as usual from the audience here, but quickly suppressed when with bitter, angry gesture he batters out his cigarette in the ashtray and with fierce jerky gestures writes and completes a new letter.]

Enter LADY MANNINGTREE *through the French windows, carrying a flat raffia basket containing freshly cut roses and delphiniums. She goes to down right, places basket on table.*

LADY MANNINGTREE. I've never known the delphiniums so heavenly as this year, Freddie. The soft blues and mauves. No wonder the dear Queen . . . (*Moves up right to collect in turn a small can of water and two vases.*) Now if you want something lovely to paint!

88

The subtlety of these colours (*begins to arrange the flowers in the vases.*) Well, have you finished? (*He waves the completed note towards her.*)

FREDDIE. Here! You've got what you want.

LADY MANNINGTREE. My dear boy! Have you quite lost your manners? (*After hesitation walks upstage to him.*) I'm not surprised. You can't touch pitch. . . . (*Takes the note and reads it.*) 'I've always known that if I was to be serious as an artist I couldn't let myself fall in love for many years to come. That's why I'm writing to you now. . . .' Serious as an artist? You have the most ingenious way of putting things.

FREDDIE. It happens to be true.

LADY MANNINGTREE *shrugs her shoulders.*

LADY MANNINGTREE. My dear boy, we're all delighted that you enjoy painting, but the vital point was that she was quite impossible. A provincial dancing school teacher. Thank goodness, we saw her in time. Even your father . . .

FREDDIE. Father's manners with Violet were perfect.

LADY MANNINGTREE. As if that helped. Anyhow, you've done the sensible thing. And you're looking very handsome, too. That scarlet dressing-gown suits you. It's the greatest absurdity to think that scarlet should only be worn by dark people. (*She puts her hand on his shoulder.*) Dear Boy!

FREDDIE (*shaking her hand off him*). Oh for God's sake Mother. I'm your son, not your lover.

From the audience, as usual, a shocked intake of breath, while LADY MANNINGTREE *walks deliberately and with great dignity to her flower arranging. As often, one or two bursts of applause from Alma Grayson devotees.*

LADY MANNINGTREE (*in casual, conversational tones*). I've got a fascinating part for this weekend, Freddie – the Cantripps, Lady Celia, The Wickendens, Francis Morell, Sybil Stutterford . . .

FREDDIE. Francis Morell?

LADY MANNINGTREE. Yes. You admire him so much.

FREDDIE. He's only our greatest painter. How did you manage to persuade him?

LADY MANNINGTREE. Oh, I have my little methods. I haven't been a hostess for twenty years. . . .

FREDDIE You're wonderful.

LADY MANNINGTREE (*beaming*). They seem like daubs to me. However . . . I wanted it to be a surprise. You deserve a reward for doing what I asked you.

FREDDIE *scowls*.

LADY MANNINGTREE. Oh, and I've asked the Carnaby girl. (*She looks to see the effect of this. He shows no interest.*) She's very pretty, Freddie.

FREDDIE. And the Carnabys are the right sort of family to marry into. That's it, isn't it?

LADY MANNINGTREE. Who said anything about marriage? Really, you young people today sound more like Victorians sometimes. Flirt with her, my dear boy, amuse yourself. Why at your age I broke a different young man's heart at every houseparty. But then we were civilised. . . before that dreadful war.

FREDDIE. And Douggie Lord? Is he coming?

LADY MANNINGTREE. Oh, I expect so. I really hardly notice him.

FREDDIE. Then you won't notice his not being there.

LADY MANNINGTREE. What do you mean? (*She stands with a vase of roses in her hand.*)

FREDDIE. Simply this. (*He takes out of his wallet and waves a sheet of a letter at her. She gives a little scream and drops the vase of roses*) . . .

ANGUS WILSON
No Laughing Matter

90

So That's The Way You Like It

This is played with great vigour at tremendous speed in the modern Shakespeare style. The characters wear various period hats as required. Enter PETER *right.*

PETER. Sustain we now description of a time
　　When petty lust and overweening tyranny
　　Offend the ruck of state.
　　Thus fly we now, as oft with Phoebus did
　　Fair Asterope, unto proud Flanders Court.
　　Where is the warlike Warwick,
　　Like to the mole that sat on Hector's brow,
　　Fairset for England and for war!

Enter JOHN *and* ALAN *on the rostrum.*

JON. And so we bid you welcome to our Court,
　　Fair Cousin Albany and you our sweetest Essex
　　Take this my hand, and you fair Essex this
　　And with this bond we'll cry anon
　　And shout Jack Cock of London to the Foe.
　　Approach your ears and kindly bend your conscience to my piece,
　　Our ruddy scouts to me this hefty news have brought:
　　The naughty English, expecting now some pregnance in our plan,
　　Have with some haughty purpose
　　Bent Aeolis unto the service of their sail.
　　So even now, while we to the wanton lute do strut,
　　Is Brutish Bolingbroke bent fair upon
　　Some fickle circumstance.

ALAN *and* PETER. Some fickle circumstance.

JON. Get thee to Gloucester, Essex. Do thee to Wessex, Exeter,
　　Fair Albany to Somerset must eke his route
　　And Scroup do you to Westmoreland, where shall bold York
　　Enrouted now for Lancaster, with forces of our Uncle Rutland,
　　Enjoin his standard with sweet Norfolk's host.

91

Fair Sussex, get thee to Warwicksbourne,
And there, with frowning purpose, tell our plan
To Bedford's tilted ear, that he shall press
With most insensate speed
And join his warlike effort to bold Dorset's side.
I most royally shall now to bed,
To sleep off all the nonsense I've just said.

Exit on rostrum.
All re-enter as rude mechanicals.

JON. Is it botched up then, Master Puke?

ALAN. Aye marry and is, good Master Snot.

DUDLEY. 'Tis said our Master, the Duke, hath contrived some
naughtiness against his son, the King.

PETER. Aye, and it doth confound our merry-making.

JON. What say you, Master Puke? I am for Lancaster, and that's to say
for good shoe leather.

PETER. Come speak, good Master Puke, or hath the leather blocked up
thy tongue?

DUDLEY. Why then go trippingly upon thy laces, good Grit?

PETER. Art leather laces thy undoing?

DUDLEY. They shall undo many a fair boot this day.

ALL. Come. Let's to our rural revel and with our song enchant our
King.

ALL *exit.*
Re-enter ALAN and DUDLEY.

DUDLEY *(Sings).*
Oh death his face my shroud hath hid
And Lethe drowned my poor love's soul
So flee we now to Pluto's realm
And in his arms shall I grow old.

ALAN. Wise words, in mouths of fools do oft themselves belie.
   Good fool – shall Essex prosper?

DUDLEY. Aye, prosper.

ALAN. Say you – prosper, fool?

DUDLEY. Aye, prosper.

ALAN. Marry then, methinks we'll prosper. And saying prosper do we
   say to cut the knot which crafty nature hath within our bowels
   locked up. But soft and who comes here?

Enter PETER on right.

PETER. Oh good my Lord, unstop your ear and yet
   Prepare to yield the optic tear to my experience.
   Such news I bring as only can crack ope
   The casket of thy soul.
   Not six miles hence
   There grows an oak whose knotty thews
   Engendered in the bosky wood doth raise itself
   Most impudent towards the solstice sun,
   So saying did there die and dying so did say.

ALAN. God! this was most gravely underta'en
   And underta'en hath Essex gravely answered it.
   Why then we'll muster and to the field of battle go
   And unto them our English sinews show.

Exit. Smoke. PETER and JON enter with swords.

JON. Why then was this encounter nobly entertained
   And so by steel shall this our contest now be buckled up.
   Come, sir. Let's to it.

PETER. Let's to it.
   Good steel, thou shalt thyself in himself thyself embowel.

JON. Come sir.

They fight.

Ah, ha, a hit!

PETER. No, sir, no hit, a miss! Come, sir, art foppish i' the mouth.

JON. Art more fop in the mouth than fop in the steel.

Fight again. PETER *'hits'* JON.

JON. Oh God, fair cousin, thou hast done me wrong.

Dies.

Now is steel twixt gut and bladder interposed.

PETER. Oh saucy Worcester, dost thou lie so still?

Enter ALAN.

ALAN. Now hath mortality her tithe collected
And sovereign Albany to the worms his course committed.
Yet weep we not; this fustian life is short
Let's on to Pontefract to sanctify our court.

Fade out.

ALAN BENNETT, PETER COOK, JONATHAN MILLER, DUDLEY MOORE
Beyond the Fringe

THE
GOOD GUIDE
GUIDE

Travelogue

High in the hills of England's historic Ely island, near historic Sherwood Forest, home of Walt Disney's Richard Todd, stands the historic University of Cambridge in the county of Cambridgeshire, bordered on all sides by Oxfordshire, Grantchester and Girtonshire. It is generally agreed that Cambridge, which takes its name from Cambridge, Massachusetts, home of our own historic Harvard University, was founded in 1066, though some claim it was as early as the Eleventh Century.

Cambridge has many royal colleges. Here we see Queens' College, known as the Rex, and King's College, known as the Backs. A royal city indeed . . . .

Here in the River Grantchester we see undergraduates in rowboats who are known as punters on account of they have flat bottoms and their proximity to Newmarket, otherwise known as Ascot, where the historic Grand National has been run over the River Styx since its inauguration in 1066. Here it was the Sir Rupert Brooke, the Immortal Bard, who later became Archbishop of Canterbury, wrote his historic Ode to a nightingale – Florence – in 1492 when he sighted the Armada, which is now being filmed in Cinemascope by Cecil B. de Mille, an American citizen. Here too we see the historic River Cam, home of the historic boat race. In the historic olden days, three men in a boat used to row from Oxford to Cambridge via Bletchley.

LESLIE BRICUSSE, FREDERIC RAPHAEL AND TONY BECHER
Out of the Blue (Footlights Revue)

from *The Good Food Guide*

THE THREE JOLLY GALLSTONES, W8

'Memorable muffins', says one enthusiastic inspector. Mrs Rhomboid still treads her own grapes, but do go properly dressed, since Major Rhomboid insists on regimental ties, and no smoking before the loyal toast . . . .

ROBERT ROBINSON

Swindon, Wiltshire
19 Edworth Road
Mr and Mrs Grayson
41%

First reports of this middle-aged couple were not good, but since inclusion in the guide last year their standards have improved. Though Mr Grayson remains rather dull, his wife is well worth a visit if you're in the neighbourhood.

Swindon, Wiltshire
21 Edworth Road
Mr & Mrs Rogers, Brianette & Granny
69%

A pleasant little family, Mr and Mrs Rogers are cheerful despite financial difficulties and always good for a chat. Brianette is a well-developed eighteen-year-old and granny is deaf. Avoid the back sitting-room.

Worthing, Sussex
88 Rockery Crescent
Mr & Mrs Potter
18%

An appalling couple, rude and short-tempered. Their kitchen is painted a frightful yellow and Mr Potter is an uncompromising Marxist.

Bletchley, Bedfordshire
6B The Flats
Doreen & Arthur Henbison
80%

At last what Bletchley has lacked for years, a really exciting couple. Arthur is an ex-hypnotist, and Doreen in the WAAF. They introduced wife-swapping to the flats four years ago and now it's hard to get in. Must book – especially at weekends.

MONTY PYTHON
The Brand New Monty Python Papperbok

Some Country Saws

When May wind blows
All nature speeds.
When husband mows
'Tis wife who weeds.

Pigs will fly and cows will speak
When shears re-sharpened last a week.

ALAN COREN

Woodworm Tuesday

On Woodworm Tuesday (2nd after Insolvency Sunday, and the first Tuesday of Spring) the traditional Estate Agents' Race is held in villages and hamlets throughout England. Although the origins of this colourful rural event are lost in the mists of chicanery, many anthropologists believe it commemorates the sale in AD 834, after much haggling, of Aelfthrith Cottage, derelict home of the Idiot of Picester, to a merchant of London. As soon as the Idiot took possession of the money and the merchant occupation of the house, the roof, so the story goes, fell in, the doors dropped off, the cesspool overflowed, the foundations sank, and the woodworm belching the last of the genuine oak beams, immediately 'felle upon ye marchaunte and devowred hym hole' (*Chronicle of Mercia,* cap XVII).

Whatever its folk heritage, the Race itself is a delightfully engaging spectacle: local Estate Agents are required to run the traditional Stonesthrow to the Station, tossing as they run a colour print of a fully modernised thatched cottage standing in two acres of unspoilt woodland, and crying 'FIVE HUNDRED POUNDS OR NEAR OFFER! FIVE HUNDRED POUNDS OR NEAR OFFER! The winner is given as his prize the first media executive of the season to arrive from Knightsbridge, who is directed to the winner's offices by the village Reeve and attendant Virgins of the Parish.

ALAN COREN
Encyclopaedia of New English Folklore

Rhubarb

As soon as the young shoots begin to appear cover them up with flower-pots, drain-pipes, or anything else that has a hyphen to let the air in. After a week or two, when they are starting to put forth leaves, drench them with quick-lime and replace the covers with the airholes bunged up. If this treatment is not successful, try stamping on them with hob-nailed boots or use the light roller. Very stubborn cases should be uprooted and burnt.

H.F. ELLIS
So This Is Science

Britain As She Is Visit

INTRODUCEMENT

Well come to England! Here you shall find the spirit of a nation ancient and with a march of ghosts from Stonehenge and the celtic dreams of druid (see the hurl of their stones on Salisburg Plain!), to the pulsing jet-Britannia and the spurting life that jumps in her efflorent cities; a modern bustling. Also, the calm and peace of her beautiful lands with bushy hedge; Kent hipfields, and many gardens of bloomer! Leafed Warwickshire! Bleary moors, when the curlews boom in the wind, and the larks song in the sky, as it was said by the famed poet, Percy Bt Sshelley! Or the famose Vale of Eves Ham known as the 'merry blossom time'!

You shall find tradition-moats, in every part castles and dainty thatched cottages which can all sing its historique of England; she is ancient democracy and parlimentsmother of all oldest. As their great poet Shakespeare himself did:

This royal throne of kinks set in the silver tea

But you want a big information of her culture and 'bottles long ago', even for tourist who is coming already in a package for its vacancy. A hasty three hundred persons exalting from a Jambo Jet as much as luxury passenger; he can leaf the impression of Old England as a stamp on wax in his head, to know a little of her tale and how it was made.

May be to visitors the patchwerk of her landmark Britain is all one loof, a wholemeat, you may seem it was a same people for the centuries. But not! Such would be a snarl of mistake. Perhaps too much is to err in the picture of English man of Queen Victoria time with stiff upper lid and top hat, safe as Bank of England and his Empire, so like a marble!

But true is other. Here also was melting-pot of races. Here also came the inwader in successes! A stew of races to bubble already, before the Normal Conquest! Battle of Hastings is 1066, a veritable watermark in England. Now come the French Chevaliers which inject their darling manners in to the rough Saxons. So you may always see a pendule in the English character; bright and heavy, light and grave, warm and jellied. Even the Civil War (1644) was different! The Cavalier (laughing) and Roundhead (square).

Changing of the Gourd

Here is the gelded past of romance! Every day like a flicker of marital dash, a traffic stop near Buckingham. The Horses jingle past and the band thrall your blood with many brasses. At Horse Guards 11 am, Buckingham Palace it is the footmen marching (11.30) but note if the Royal Flag is not on its pike then you must amend to St James Palace up the Mall. There you can see the celebrity guardsmen with the grand bearskins and scarlet, or Life Gurds with vast boots and plums in the wind on their changers, truly a vestige to tangle your spine!

Welcome to London! Have fur in their city!

PAUL JENNINGS

More Saws

He who has the biggest feet will cover most ground.

ALISON PRINCE

If there's no lead in your pencil you don't need a rubber.

J.A. SMITH

101

A five-pound note has no effect in a penny slot machine.

R. S. JAFFRAY

Your elbow's near your mouth, but you can't suck it.

R. ROSSETTI

There is no second-class post in Heaven.

MARTIN FAGG

The Consumer's Guide to Religion

JUDAISM

This is the oldest religion we tested. Its small number of users, thirteen million, is deceptive, since many large and powerful subsidiaries derive from it.

A What do you put into it?
Belief in one only God.

Several dos and don'ts.
Never prepare milk and meat in the same dish.
Do not work between sunset on Friday and sunset on Saturday.
And you must cut off the foreskins of your male children.

B What do you get out of it?
Membership of the oldest club in the world.
Prayers and advice are tailored to fit most consumer crises and can also be newly bespoke.
You are one of the Chosen People.
This gives confidence, and we particularly liked the guarantee of eternal life through the Messiah who will take responsibility for all your guilt when he arrives.

C What does it cost?
In crockery alone the expense is fantastic. Plus the wages of a reliable gentile to run the business between sunset on Friday and sunset on Saturday.

Infertility is the only ground for divorce. We did not try to obtain one.

PROTESTANTISM

Protestantism is a breakaway from the Roman parent organisation.

Two main brands are available: the big Church of England, or the Nonconformist economy pack.

What do you put into it?

Belief that the Queen should be Head of the Church;

Belief that the Prime Minister should appoint the Archbishop of Canterbury.

And belief in God.

What do you get out of it?

Independence.

How much does it cost?

Surprisingly little.

We found no difficulty in obtaining a divorce.

In choosing the **Best Buy,** we rejected Islam as a cut-price form of Judaism; and we liked Buddhism, but the product doesn't travel well and thrives best in a warm climate. Judaism we thought frankly unsafe. We recommend that unless you have it from birth you would do better to avoid this product.

If you can afford it, Roman Catholicism with its Continental line plus international performance is well worth having. But we suggest you should think carefully before deciding on it because it's by no means trouble-free.

The attraction of the Church of England lies in its democratic spirit. If you want transubstantiation you can have transubstantiation. If you don't want transubstantiation then you don't have to have it. If you want mass you can have mass. If you want immaculate conception you can have that too. But nobody will force you to have it if you don't want it.

And the church speaks to you in English .... It's a jolly friendly faith. If you are one, there's no onus on you to make anyone else join. In fact no-one need ever know. And it's pretty fair on the whole too. With some of these products that we've mentioned – Roman Catholicism and Judaism for instance – you start guilty from the off.

But the Church of England is English. On the whole you start pretty well innocent and they've got to prove you guilty. All in all we think you get a jolly good little faith for a very moderate outlay and we have no hesitation in proclaiming it the Best Buy.

ROBERT GILLESPIE & CHARLES LEWSON
That Was The Week That Was

In The Air

The Mouse Problem

PRESENTER. This week *The World Around Us* examines the growing social phenomenon of Mice and Men. What is it that makes a man want to be a mouse?

INTERVIEWEE. Well. It's not a question of wanting to be a mouse. Er. It just sort of happens to you. All of a sudden you realise, well that's what you want to be.

PRESENTER. When did you first notice these, shall we say, 'tendencies'?

INTERVIEWEE. Well, I was about seventeen, and some mates and me went along to a party and, you know, we had a lot to drink, and then well some of the fellows started handing cheese around, and just out of curiosity I tried a bit. And that was that.

PRESENTER. And what else did these fellows do?

INTERVIEWEE. Well, some of them started dressing up as mice a bit, and then when they got the mouse costumes on they started squeaking.

PRESENTER. Was that all?

INTERVIEWEE. That was all. Yeah.

PRESENTER. And what was your reaction?

INTERVIEWEE. Well, I was shocked. But gradually I come to feel that I was more at ease when I was with other mice . . . .

MONTY PYTHON
The Worst of Monty Python's Flying Circus

Start the Year with Richard Baker

BAKER. Good morning, and welcome to 1980. The theme of today's programme is beginnings – starting things again, making resolutions – and what better time than the start of a new year to talk about, uh, that sort of thing. In the studio we have Derek Robinson and we'll be asking him if British Leyland will be getting a good first-time start in this new decade. Fritz Spiegl will be looking at the opening bars of some famous musical works. Kenneth Robinson has been to the National Underwear Show at Olympia and where better to start than with foundation garments? And though he's not here yet, Anthony Blunt will be along to tell us what it's like starting a new life as Mister after so many days as a knight. (*Laughter.*) Mavis?

MAVIS NICHOLSON. Goodness, I don't think we've ever had a traitor on the programme before.

BAKER. No, quite. Now, Derek Robinson, I believe you're the author of a new book out today called *Sack Edwardes and Save British Leyland*. How did *you* spend New Year's Eve?

BLUNT. Actually, I'm Anthony Blunt.

BAKER. Oh. Then which one of us is Derek Robinson?

KENNETH ROBINSON. Not me. I've often been confused with Robert Robinson, but never with Derek. I was once, though, mistaken for Heath Robinson when I was touring with ENSA in 1943 . . . .

BAKER. Quite. Well, it seems that Derek Robinson is not here yet. Obviously he'll have to make a resolution to be punctual this year! Anthony Blunt, you're a traitor and author of a new book entitled *New Light on Eighteenth-Century Italian Architecture*. How did *you* spend New Year's Eve?

MAVIS. I wonder if I might butt in there, Richard . . . .

BAKER. Mavis Nicholson . . . .

MAVIS. . . . and say, gosh, I wonder if I would have the courage to betray my friends if it was a choice between them and my paintings, would I have the inner strength, I just don't know.

BAKER. Quite. Sir Anthony?

BLUNT. Professor.

BAKER. Quite. Mr Blunt?

BLUNT. I spent New Year's Eve quietly with a few close paintings.

BAKER. It's a curious idea, isn't it, to spend New Year's Eve as if it were some ritual? Kenneth?

KENNETH. I stayed up all evening writing my spontaneous contribution to this programme.

BAKER. Time now to hear from Fritz Spiegl on musical beginnings.

SPIEGL. We all know the famous unfinished works, but what about the unstarted ones? Did you know that Brunswick left the first movement of his 8th Symphony till last and then never wrote it? Here are the first few bars. (*Silence*.) And have you noticed how seldom we hear Wagner's overture to *Furtwängler*? That's because he wrote the opera but not the overture. Here it is in its entirety. (*Silence*.) But I could go on like this endlessly.

BAKER. Quite so. Incidentally, Fritz, have you made any resolutions?

KENNETH. Fritz isn't here, Richard. That was just a recording. Anyway, I've been to the National Underwear Show at Olympia . . . .

BAKER. Which reminds me, Kenneth – you've been to the National Underwear Show at Olympia, haven't you?

KENNETH. I certainly have . . . .

MILES KINGTON

Thought for the Day

The speaker this morning is the Reverend Daphne Pullover of the Seamen's Mission, Wolverhampton.

Good Morning. Listening to the news of all the storms which have been so widespread during the night, my mind returned to one of those odd little sayings of childhood when thunder was about. 'Don't worry,' we used to say. 'It's only God moving the furniture about.' Do you remember that? It's a nice thought, isn't it? God's furniture. I wonder what kind of furniture God would have? A sturdy oak dresser, perhaps, or a mahogany hallstand with a mirror. Would he have a bidet, I wonder? And prefer a shower to a bath? What fun it would be to be God's removal man, moving things about among his many mansions. And you know Christians tend to be a bit like that, a bit like God's removal men, moving his word from place to place.

RUSSELL DAVIES
A Day in the Life of Radio 4

Lady Minerva Throbing's Country Seat

And now John Betjeman and Arthur Negus examine the country seat of Lady Minerva Throbing at her ancestral home, Henry Hall.

BETJEMAN. Well, Arthur. We've been through the refectory and the housemaid's pantry, and now this looks to me like the smallest room in the house. It looks rather like a Priest's Hole doesn't it?

NEGUS. It does, John. But it does say 'Engaged' on it.

BETJEMAN. I shouldn't worry too much about that. I expect that's been there since the eighteenth century. Let's try . . . .

Shriek.

Good gracious! What an extraordinary sight.

NEGUS. It's an extraordinary piece, isn't it, John? It's a really remarkable . . . .

BETJEMAN. What would you say it was?

NEGUS. Well I would say it was a figurine. A seated figurine.

BETJEMAN. A rather large seated figurine. What sort of date would you put on it?

NEGUS. Well, to look at it, I'd say nineteenth – late nineteenth century.

BETJEMAN. I think you're right. Yes. I'd say you can see from the legs really. The sort of varicose-y legs – by Edmund Varicosi, who was very active – extremely active – in this part of the world.

NEGUS. He was very active on these legs. Look at these beautiful bits of fluting. I don't think I've ever seen fluted legs quite so delicately fluted.

BETJEMAN. Try running your hands up. You can just feel this wonderful workmanship. You see if you'll just come round here. Let's just have a look at the bottom. Sometimes you get some interesting sort of, you know, water marks on it . . . .

PRIVATE EYE
Record: 'Private Eye Golden Satiricals'

The Critics

CHAIRMAN. Mrs Vinegar.

MRS VINEGAR. I was bored with this play. Or whatever it is. I was bored almost from the rise of the curtain with the characters – or is characters too strong a word? – and I was even more bored by the situations they were put into.

MUSTARD. And the acting? Were you bored with the acting? I thought the cast carried it off for him exceptionally well.

PEPPER. A splendid cast.

MUSTARD. Quite exceptionally well.

MISS SALT. It was in fact an actors' play.

MUSTARD. An actors' play and of course in a way a producer's play.

CHAIRMAN. How would Mrs Vinegar feel about calling this an actors' play?

MRS VINEGAR. No. No, I thought the acting was extremely good. The production I'm less sure about, but it was quite sound. As for this being an actors' play or a producer's play, whatever that may mean, I think fifth-rate play is the only sound designation for it. No amount of talent on the stage can make a fifth-rate play into a third-rate one, although it was quite obvious that that was what they were aiming at.

CHAIRMAN. Mustard Short. Were you bored by this play?

MUSTARD. Bored, no. Exasperated at times, yes. I did, I think, suppress a mild yawn twice, but I smiled occasionally, wondered what was coming next, got annoyed and irritated fairly frequently – in fact reacted much as one does in the theatre, except for experiencing tension. There was no tension and no tears. That I think was a pity because with so much else there it would have been nice for the sake of completeness to have had those as well . . . .

N. F. SIMPSON
A Resounding Tinkle

Novel-writing Live

ANNOUNCER. And now it's time for novel-writing, which today comes from the West Country, from Dorset.

COMMENTATOR. Hello and welcome to Dorchester, where a very good crowd has turned out to watch local boy Thomas Hardy write his new novel *The Return of the Native* on this very pleasant July morning. This will be his eleventh novel and the fifth of the very popular Wessex Novels. And here he comes. Here comes Hardy, walking out towards his desk. He looks confident, he looks relaxed, very much the man in form as he acknowledges this very good-natured Bank Holiday crowd. And the crowd goes quiet now as Hardy settles himself down at the desk. Body straight, shoulders relaxed, pen held lightly but firmly in the right hand. He dips the pen in the ink – and he's off. It's the first word. But it's not a word! Oh no! It's a doodle. Way up on the top of the left-hand margin. It's a piece of meaningless scribble. And he's signed his name underneath it. Oh dear! What a disappointing start. But he's off again. And here he goes. The first word of Thomas Hardy's new novel at 10.35 on this very lovely morning – it's three letters, and it's THE . Dennis . . . .

DENNIS. Well this is true to form. No surprises there. He started five of his eleven novels to date with the definite article. We have had two of them with 'it', there's been one 'but' two 'ats' one 'on' and a 'Dolores' – though that of course was never published.

COMMENTATOR. I'm sorry to interrupt you there, Dennis, but he's crossed it out . . . .

MONTY PYTHON
Record: 'The Monty Python Instant Record Collection'

Alan Whicker Investigates a Saviour

ALAN WHICKER *appears against a wilderness background.*

WHICKER. There is a long tradition here of austere, ascetic anchorites, a bonanza of breast-beating, beatific saints seeking solitude and salvation. Goodbye the world, the flesh and the devil; hello to fasting and flagellation. But today we have something that beats all.

Pan to JESUS CHRIST.

Not a pretty sight, is it?
   Normally you wouldn't want to get downwind of a character like this. But let's take a closer look. For this son of a small-town artisan is making claims that out-Herod Herod. He's all about meditation, miracles and Messianic messages. Follow him, runs the sales pitch, and you'll be washed whiter than white. If you want your just deserts, that's what he's into – just deserts. There's barely a tree in sight. Tell me, sir, what exactly are your lonesome lucubrations in aid of?

JESUS CHRIST. Get thee behind me, Satan.

JIM McGUIGAN

Test Match Special

HENRY BLOFELD. . . . and there's no run. That's the seventh maiden over running from O'Keefe to Boycott. I think that's the first time that a left-handed spinner has bowled seven maidens running on the third day of a Test Match between England and Australia since Ernie Toshack in 1948. Wouldn't you agree, Trevor?

TREVOR BAILEY. . . . Well I remember Tony Lock had a very long spell of maidens at Old Trafford in 1956 – you remember, the game when Jim Laker got 19 wickets – but whether that was on the third day or not I can't be sure . . .

DISTANT VOICE. . . . No, it was on the fourth day, in fact, after tea.

BLOFELD. Bill Frindall tells us that it was in fact on the fourth day of the Old Trafford Test that Tony Lock bowled all those maidens . . . .

Background noise of ball being hit and applause.

TREVOR BAILEY. . . . and I think this is the first time it's been done at the Oval, at least from the Vauxhall End . . . .

BLOFELD. . . . and indeed against a side with no left-handers . . . .

Sound of ball being hit and wild applause.

BAILEY. . . . that was a very interesting observation indeed. Although I do remember there was a Pakistan side in the West Indies sometime in the sixties which had nothing but left-handers . . . .

BLOFELD. . . . you must be thinking of the 1964-5 side, with Muhammed Ahmed and Mushtaq Tandoori . . . .

VOICE IN BACKGROUND. I think that side did have one right-hander, Muhammed Muhammed, although he was off the field for most of the match.

BRIAN JOHNSTON. Thank you Bill. Bill Frindall tells us that there was in fact one right-hander in that Pakistan side at Kingston, was it Bill . . . ?

VOICE IN BACKGROUND. No, Georgetown.

JOHNSON. Oh, Bill Frindall tells me it was Georgetown.

Sound of wicket being knocked over and more applause.

Of course it's a lovely ground there at Georgetown, next to the sea. Some of us remember that famous riot which brought an end to the Test Match between England and the West Indies in 1957–8.

VOICE IN BACKGROUND. 1970–1, actually, Brian.

BAILEY. Of course seven maidens in a row is far from being a record. You will recall that great Somerset left-armer Horace Hazell once bowled no less than 21 maiden overs on the trot at Taunton . . . .

VOICE IN BACKGROUND. 21.5 overs actually.

114

BAILEY. Marvellous line-and-length bowler, Horace Hazell . . . .

Sound of pavilion collapsing.

BLOFELD. And we welcome World Service listeners with the news that Horace Hazell bowled more maiden overs consecutively than any other slow left-arm spin bowler since . . . .

PRIVATE EYE

First Performance

BBC ANNOUNCER (*filling in during non-appearance of the performers*). And now we welcome you to the Memorial Hall where we are broadcasting the first performance of a recently discovered fragment for piano and alto sackbut by the Bavarian composer Heinrich Danzig. Danzig was born in 1886 at Olsbrucke and died in Florence 10 years ago in 1957 at the age of 71. This fragment dates from 1909, when the composer was 23, and was written while he was on a holiday at Badesheim. The soloist tonight is Florence Brush, born in Danzig in 1926, when the composer was 40 years old, 31 years before his death in 1957 at the age of 71, and 17 years after the composition of this fragment in 1909 at Badesheim. Miss Brush later went to the Cockfosters School of Music in 1947, 21 years later at the age of 22, and as far as we know she is still alive. Her accompanist tonight is Feruccio Brangani, born in Cockfosters in 1927, when the composer was 41 and the soloist was nine months old, 18 years after this work was written in 1909 at Badesheim and 40 years before it is being performed tonight in the Memorial Hall, which was built in 1950, 17 years ago, 74 years after the composer was born, 34 years after the soloist was born, 41 years after this work was composed in 1909 at Badesheim and 2 years before my first wedding anniversary. The man selling the tickets is Albert Buttermold, born in 1904 – one year after . . . 1903 . . . . And I am afraid that is all we have time for from tonight's concert, so I return you back to the studio. Goodnight.

JOHN GOULD and DAVID WOOD
Four Degrees Over

Whinfrey's Last Case

An elegant London square. Time: the Present.

A VERY FAMOUS PERSONALITY *contemplates the hustle and bustle of London, then turns impressively and talks to a camera which follows his every move.*

VERY FAMOUS PERSONALITY. Good evening . . . I want to ask you, if I may tonight, to join me in an experiment. An experiment to turn back time, to suspend belief in the here and now of a busy city, and to join me in the past. . . . Come with me now. (*He starts to move leading the camera with him*) . . . to a London before two wars, when this house . . .

. . . he indicates a smart London residence just as a delivery van draws up against the kerb outside the house, completely blocking the VERY FAMOUS AND CHARISMATIC PERSONALITY *from view. The* VERY FAMOUS PERSONALITY *continues to drone on obliviously, as the van's hand-brake is applied and the engine rattles noisily to a halt.*

. . . was the London home of one of the most powerful men of this century. Through this elegant doorway . . .

An anoraked and stop-watched BBC PRODUCTION ASSISTANT *rushes out from behind camera and across the road to ask the van to move. She runs right across the path of an oncoming Vauxhall Viva de luxe, which skids to a halt with a screech of brakes.*

VERY FAMOUS PERSONALITY. . . . came and went the greatest names of pre-war days.

The PA *approaches the driver, a* MEAT PORTER, *indicates the camera and asks him to move on.*

. . . Kaisers, Tsars and Cabinet Ministers stood at these very windows . . .

The MEAT PORTER *looks at camera, gets down from cab, and gives a cheerful nod and a wink as he goes to the back of the van.*

116

. . . and on that balcony you see above me stood the King of England himself.

The driver of the Vauxhall has now joined the helpless PA. *The driver (a* TRAVELLER IN UNDERWEAR *from the Midlands) argues with the* PA *and points out how he nearly hit her.*

The MEAT PORTER *appears carrying a side of pig over his shoulder.*

The owner of this quietly elegant residence was the legendary Gerald Whinfrey, the man who saved governments and ended wars . . . in an era when individual bravery and courage were still valued highly . . . .

A terrible skid and rending crash is heard off. The Viva de luxe jerks forward. The TRAVELLER IN UNDERWEAR *looks round in horror. His car has obviously been rammed. The* MEAT PORTER *is now quite blatantly waving at camera.*

This is where our journey back in time must begin.

There is a sound of a police siren off. Slamming of doors, the MEAT PORTER *gets into his cab and then out again. He performs a little dance for the camera, winking and mugging a lot. Halfway through a neat pas-de-deux an* OFFICER OF THE LAW *approaches, but before he can raise a truncheon the* MEAT PORTER *ceases his performance and nips smartly back into the cab.*

. . . Take one last lingering look at this building and imagine yourselves back in the year 1913, the year of wars and rumours of wars, the year that saw the extraordinary tale (*The lorry drives off. The* VERY FAMOUS AND CHARISMATIC PERSONALITY *turns, at the crescendo of his oratory, to camera.*) of Whinfrey's Last Case . . . .

TERRY JONES AND MICHAEL PALIN
More Ripping Yarns

A Strong Wind in the Balearics
Round Britain Quiz

CLOUGH. Well now, Irene and John Julius, here's your question. What kind of trio would you get from a blob of pistachio, the thirteenth letter of the alphabet, and a strong wind in the Balearics?

NORWICH. Well, I say. This is very difficult.

THOMAS. I'll say it is.

NORWICH. Oh, dear. I haven't got a clue. (*Short pause – to try and convince listeners that he hasn't. We are not fooled.*) Unless . . . unless this 'blob of pistachio' is a reference to the Bavarian Charcoal-Cutters' Rebellion of 1756. Is it?

CLOUGH. Yes it is, John Julius. Spot on. Well done.

NORWICH. Only of course, as Hotchkiss proved recently, it wasn't really pistachio that started it; it was actually a rudimentary kind of vegetable marrow.

THOMAS. Was it really? How fascinating!

CLOUGH. Bang on, John Julius, well done. Now then, how about the thirteenth letter of the alphabet?

THOMAS. That's 'M'.

CLOUGH. Yes it is, Irene. Well done. Well done.

NORWICH. Is this a reference to Savonarola?

CLOUGH. Absolutely, John Julius. Savonarola it is.

NORWICH. Shortly before the Great Recant of 1541, he called for a large dish of scrambled eggs which were coded on the prison menu as 'M' because of the Neapolitan slang for eggs, which was 'uova'.

CLOUGH. Quite right. Quite right.

THOMAS. But 'uova' doesn't begin with an 'M'.

NORWICH. No, the prison chef had a speech impediment.

CLOUGH. He certainly did. That's just what he had. A speech impediment. Well done. And the strong wind in the Balearics?

NORWICH. Surely this is Bismarck.

CLOUGH. Yes it is.

THOMAS. The treaty of 1891 and the so-called War of the Billiard Balls.

CLOUGH. That's it. Absolutely right. So, put them all together and what kind of trio do you get?

NORWICH. Bavaria . . . eggs . . . Bismarck . . . this isn't a Polish delicatessen, is it?

CLOUGH. No it isn't.

THOMAS (*hesitant*). Could it be the 1969 Young Persons Offenders Act, then?

CLOUGH. Yes that's it, Irene. Well done, the 1969 Act is is. Well done. Quite right. Well, you sailed through that with no difficulty at all; but I think I'm only going to give you $1\frac{1}{2}$ points. Well done . . . .

ROB BUCKMAN
Jogging From Memory

Laying Down The Law

Rex v. Haddock: Is It A Free Country?

The Court of Criminal Appeal considered to-day an important case involving the rights and liberties of the subject, if any.

LORD LIGHT, LCJ. This is in substance an appeal by an appellant appealing *in statu quo* against a decision of the West London Half-Sessions, confirming a conviction by the magistrates of South Hammersmith sitting in Petty Court some four or five years ago. The ancillary proceedings have included two hearings *in sessu* and an appeal rampant on the case, as a result of which the record was ordered to be torn up and the evidence reprinted backwards *ad legem*. With these transactions, however, the Court need not concern itself, except to observe that, as for our learned brother Mumble, whose judgments we have read with diligence and something approaching to nausea, it were better that a millstone should be hanged round his neck and he be cast into the uttermost depths of the sea.

The present issue is one of comparative simplicity. That is to say, the facts of the case are intelligible to the least-instructed layman, and the only persons utterly at sea are those connected with the law. But *factum clarum, jus nebulosum,* or, 'the clearer the facts the more dubious the law'. What the appellant did in fact is simple and manifest, but what offence, if any, he has committed in law is a question of the gravest difficulty.

What he did in fact was to jump off Hammersmith Bridge in the afternoon of August 18th, 1922, during the Hammersmith Regatta. The motive of the act is less clear. A bystander named Snooker, who, like himself, was watching the regatta from the bridge, has sworn in evidence that he addressed the appellant in the following terms: 'Betcher a pound you won't jump over, mate,' that the appellant, who had had a beer or (as he frankly admitted) two, replied in these words: 'Bet you I will, then,' after which pronouncement he removed his coat, handed it to the man Snooker, climbed on to the rail, and jumped into the water below, which, as was sworn by Professor Rugg of the Royal Geographical Society, forms part of the River Thames. The appellant is a strong swimmer,

123

and, on rising to the surface, he swam in a leisurely fashion towards the Middlesex bank. When still a few yards from the shore, however, he was overtaken by a river police boat, the officers in which had observed his entrance into the water and considered it their duty to rescue the swimmer. They therefore took him, unwilling, it appears, into their boat, and landed him. He was then arrested by an officer of the Metropolitan Police engaged in controlling the crowds who had gathered to watch the regatta, was taken to the police station and subsequently charged before the magistrates, when he was ordered to pay a fine of two pounds.

The charges were various, and it is difficult to say upon which of them the conviction was ultimately based. The appellant was accused of:

(A) Causing an obstruction
(B) Being drunk and disorderly
(C) Attempting to commit suicide
(D) Conducting the business of a street bookmaker
(E) (Under the Navigation Acts) endangering the lives of mariners
(F) (Under the Port of London Authority By-laws) interfering with an authorized regatta.

It may be said at once that in any case no blame whatever attaches to the persons responsible for the framing of these charges, who were placed in a most difficult position by the appellant's unfortunate act. It is a principle of English law that a person who appears in a police court has done something undesirable, and citizens who take it upon themselves to do unusual actions which attract the attention of the police should be careful to bring these actions into one of the recognised categories of crimes and offences, for it is intolerable that the police should be put to the pains of inventing reasons for finding them undesirable.

The appellant's answer to the charges severally were these. He said that he had not caused an obstruction by doing an act which gathered a crowd together, for a crowd had already gathered to watch the regatta, both on the bridge and on the banks. He said that although he had had one beer, or even two, he was neither drunk nor disorderly. Snooker and others about him swore that he showed no signs of either condition when on the bridge, and it was powerfully argued that the fact of a man jumping from a high place into water was not *prima facie* evidence of intoxication. Witnesses were called to show that a man at Bournemouth had constantly jumped from the pier in flames without any such suggestion, and indeed with the connivance of the police and in the presence of the Mayor and Council. In the alternative, the appellant said that, assuming that he was intoxicated before his immersion, which he denied, he must obviously have been, and in fact was, sober when arrested, which is admitted; while the river police in cross-examination were unable to say that he was swimming in a disorderly manner, or with any unseemly splashes or loud cries such as might have supported an accusation of riotous behaviour.

In answer to the charge of attempted suicide the appellant said (a) that only the most unconventional suicide would select for his attempt an occasion on which there were numerous police boats and other craft within view, (b) that it is not the natural action of a suicide to remove his coat before the fatal plunge, and (c) that his first act on rising to the surface was in fact to swim methodically to a place of safety.

As to the betting charge, the appellant said that he had never made a bet in his life; no other person but Snooker heard or saw anything of the transaction; and since Snooker, who on his own showing had lost the wager, confessed in cross-examination that he had not in fact passed any money to the appellant, but, on the contrary, had walked off quietly with the appellant's coat, the credit of this witness was a little shaken, and this charge may be said to have fallen to the ground. The appellant himself said that he did what he did (to use his own curious phrase) 'for fun'.

Finally, as to the Navigation and Port of London Authority Acts, the appellant called overwhelming evidence to prove that, at the time of his immersion, no race was actually in progress and no craft or vessel was within fifty yards from the bridge.

But in addition to these particular answers, all of which in my judgment have substance, the appellant made the general answer that this was a free country and a man can do what he likes if he does nobody any harm. And with that observation the appellant's case takes on at once an entirely new aspect. If I may use an expression which I have used many times before in this Court, it is like the thirteenth stroke of a crazy clock, which not only is itself discredited but casts a shade of doubt over all previous assertions. For it would be idle to deny that a man capable of that remark would be capable of the grossest forms of licence and disorder. It cannot be too clearly understood that this is *not* a free country, and it will be an evil day for the legal profession when it is. The citizens of London must realise that there is almost nothing they are allowed to do. *Prima facie* all actions are illegal, if not by Act of Parliament, by Order in Council; and if not by Order in Council, by Departmental or Police Regulations, or By-laws. They may not eat where they like, drink where they like, walk where they like, drive where they like, sing where they like, or sleep where they like. And least of all may they do unusual actions 'for fun'. People must not do things for fun. We are not here for fun. There is no reference to fun in any Act of Parliament. If anything is said in this Court to encourage a belief that Englishmen are entitled to jump off bridges for their own amusement the next thing to go will be the Constitution. For these reasons, therefore, I have come to the conclusion that this appeal must fail. It is not for me to say what offence the appellant has committed, but I am satisfied that he has committed *some* offence, for which he has been most properly punished.

MUDD, J., said that in his opinion the appellant had polluted a watercourse under the Public Health Act, 1875.

ADDER, J., concurred. He thought that the appellant had attempted to pull down a bridge, under the Malicious Damage Act, 1861.

   The appeal was dismissed.

NOTE – See also *HM Customs and Excise v. Bathbourne Literary Society* for the law relating to fun and laughter.

A.P. HERBERT
Uncommon Law

In Layman's Terms

A devise of incorporeal rent secks which subsist in subwrit of coignybar, I do not mind telling you may rank for apportionment with appendant seignmoigns du petit playsaunce, quit-writs of *cestui que cave* and re-entered copy-warrants of grand attainder.

   It was once urged (v. Bract, fo. 87a, 207a, Vinogradoff Hist. E.L. xvii Reg. v Shaughnessy et al.) that the devise of a rent-charged easement held in frankalchaise-a-moins with mesne bars inquoted was a lawful devise *having regard to fraundpuissaunce of charterfee.* Held by Pallas C.B. that

... devises charged with consolidated quodwrits of quit-bar or seigny-poke subsist thereafter in fee of grossplaysaunce, notwithstanding all copyholds of mesnemanor, socagemoign, interfee, mortlease, grand bastardy in copygross, sub-escheats of scutage *quousque,* refeoffed disseisor of sub-seisin in seignyfrankalpuis and vivmain of copycharged serjaunty.

To-day, this may seem a somewhat staid – even a technical – pronouncement. Yet when it was made it was regarded by the Irish people as the most stirring vindication of their immemorial right to quit-scutage and sochemaunce – indeed, a wider charter of democratic self-determination than the Local Government Act of 1898.

MYLES NA GOPALEEN
The Best of Myles

Whereas

(A) The Author of this Deed is at present seised in fee simple and in stupor tremens by the process of moving house.

(B) The Author is of sound mind SAVE THAT the Vendor of the first part and the Mortgagee of the second part and the Assignor of the third part and the Leaseholder of the fourth part and the Lessee of the fifth part and the Curtainor of the sixth part and the Carpetee of the seventh part and the Gasholder of the eighth part HAVE AGREED to cover all floors walls tables and other surfaces in the present residence of the Author with three coats of prime quality LEGAL DOCUMENTS.

(C) The aforementioned legal documents are close carpeted throughout with verbiage of a tasteful period character.

Provided that
A space shall be kept clear among the said verbiage to accommodate an Excise Stamp charged at NOT MORE than one third of the Government's current defence expenditure.

And wherethemore
(A) For a consideration the Solicitors of the aforementioned parties have agreed to join in these deeds SEEING THAT no aforementioned party would really go with a swing without them.

(B) Given the slightest additional consideration the Solicitors' Solicitors and the Solicitors' Solicitors' Solicitors would doubtless also join in both in fee simple and fee compound.

Provided that
The aforementioned partygiver (hereinafter called 'the Mortgaged Soul') shall not be responsible for maintaining more than half the country's legal profession at any one time.

And wherewithstanding
IN THE EVENT of a person being both Vendor of one property and Vendee of another it is required by Logic that the Market cannot be unfavourable to him in both capacities.

EXCEPT THAT in the case of the Author the Market shall be guaranteed to be permanently against him whether as Vendor Vendee or Vendsoever.

And whereasmuchas
(A) The Friends of the Author (hereinafter called Christopher and Lavinia Crumble) bought purchased or became seised of their demesne two years ago for the sum of ONE THOUSAND POUNDS (£1,000).

(B) The value of the said demesne THEREUPON without let or hindrance and without prejudice to the liberal reputation of the aforesaid Christopher and Lavinia Crumble rose to TEN THOUSAND POUNDS (£10,000).

(C) This being achieved in part by the application of two coats of pale mauve paint by the said Christopher Crumble and in part by the removal of all adjacent tenants of immoral or drunken habits or small means and their replacement by new tenants of immoral or drunken habits and more substantial means.

And wheremoresoever
Even those Friends of the Author known as Horace and Doris Morris ordinarily situate in the same boat as the Author and generally supposed by the Author to be at least as fee simple about these matters as himself have acquired a residence the size of a small cathedral for A SONG (I Sng.).

And wherewithas
(A) In contradistinction to the Morrises and Crumbles the Author of

128

this Deed (or Doer or Deedee) shall entertain all reasonable certainty that he will hereinafter be known as the Deedled or Done.

(B) The Author shall hereupon feel himself personally responsible for the maintenance in good condition of the Property Market heretofore known as the Property Racket.

(C) The Author shall be absolutely entitled to feel ground floor flat by the whole business.

Now it is agreed
The Author shall have in perpetuity the peaceful enjoyment of the dirty end of the stick.

Now this deed
WITNESSETH as follows:
The Author solemnly covenants with himself that notwithstanding overcrowding dilapidation infestation sudden enrichment sudden impoverishment conjugal representations or the purchase by Horace and Doris Morris of a royal palace in good order for fifteen shillings and sixpence NOR EVEN WITHSTANDING unemployment need and hunger among the Legal Profession HE SHALL before he contemplates moving house again meditate deeply upon this document for three calendar months following the first full moon after the penultimate Quarter Day of the next Leap Year but one.

In witness whereof the party hereto sets hereunder his exhausted hand.

MICHAEL FRAYN
On The Outskirts

Law Report: Court of Appeal

Why Frog Has Legal Right To Sue Trade Union

Grenouille v National Union of Seamen
Before Lord Denning, Master of the Rolls, Lord Justice Lawton and Lord Justice Eveleigh.

A frog was a person in law and accordingly had the necessary *locus standi* to bring injunction proceedings before the courts, especially where the respondent was a wicked and irresponsible trade union. The Court of Appeal so held in allowing an appeal by Mr Grenouille, a frog, of Ball's Pond, against a decision by Mr Justice Woolf refusing to grant an injunction restraining the National Union of Seamen from mounting a picket around the appellant's pond.

Mr George Carman QC and Mr Douglas Hogg appeared for the frog. Mr Peter Taylor QC and Mr Fenton Bresler for the union.

THE MASTER OF THE ROLLS said that the appeal raised issues of profound importance to the rule of law. No less than the continued existence of the courts to protect citizens from oppression was at stake. The facts were simple. Mr Grenouille awoke one May morning to find his pond surrounded by pickets belonging to the National Union of Seamen. They were stopping the public from throwing food into the pond. The frog became ill. He was on the way to starvation. The National Association for Freedom, Enterprise, and Self-Reliance took up his case and last week, through counsel, asked a judge to order the union to remove the pickets. The union, in an affidavit to the court, said that the picket was lawful. It was 'in furtherance of a trade dispute,' it claimed, the dispute being between Sandanista guerrillas and the Nicaraguan Government over working hours and conditions. The court had no doubt that the union's action did not fall within the criteria laid down for a union to be able to claim immunity from an action in the courts.

But counsel for the union had persuaded the learned judge below that a frog had no legal right to be heard by the courts at all. Lord Denning said that he had no hesitation in adopting the opposite view. It would be a black day indeed for British justice if it were only to be available to brave men such as Mr John Gouriet and Sir Freddie Laker, and not to humble, law-abiding frogs. No-one, however lowly, was below the law. It was the court's duty to protect the weak against the strong. The decent member of the community – frog or human – who has fallen victim to injustice at the hands of dangerous, unchristian, wicked, and irresponsible conglomerations of power, of which trade unions were, together with the Home Office, the main examples, must have the right to seek help from the courts, and the courts must offer a remedy. For them to do otherwise would be to betray those revered men who, so many centuries ago, gathered in that silent meadow at Runnymede. To those who said that frogs were beyond the law, the answer was that if frogs were beyond the law, then the rule of law existed no longer. He was in no doubt that that could not be so, and that frogs, for all legal purposes, were persons able to sue and be sued in the courts of Her Majesty.

It was true, Lord Denning said, that there were six decisions of the House of Lords which appeared to be dead against that proposition. He would pay little heed to them. They seemed to him to have been all wrongly decided, and it was settled law, at any rate in his court, that decisions of the House of Lords were not binding on the Court of Appeal. But even if he were obliged to follow precedent set by that House (and, it was fair to point out, some commentators took that view) he would have no difficulty in distinguishing the facts of the present case. None of the House of Lords decisions relied on by counsel for the union referred specifically to the legal status of frogs. Their Lordships had simply not turned their minds to ranidae, and it could not be assumed that the principles which governed the legal positions of horses, prawns and budgerigars would necessarily apply to the very different circumstances of the appellant. He could not see how Mr Grenouille's case could be said to be analagous to the facts in *Red Rum v Marks and Spencer Ltd* ([1979] AC 165) where the court had refused to allow Mr Rum, a horse, to sue for fees owed to him for opening the store's Hampstead branch.

Lord Denning said that he had been conducting some researches and had found a case in point, supporting his view. It was a decision by the deputy magistrate of East Tonga (South Sea Reports, 1931-1958, p 645) prohibiting the destruction of 5,000 toads for use in a marriage ceremony. With the greatest respect to their noble Lordships, he found their reasoning less persuasive than that of the experienced Tongan magistrate.

LORD JUSTICE LAWTON said that although he had the greatest possible respect for the Master of the Rolls, he disagreed with everything he had said. Nevertheless he agreed that the appeal should be allowed. Trade Unions ought to be restrained from actions which would result in anarchy and the inevitable breakdown of parliamentary democracy.

LORD JUSTICE EVELEIGH said that the law was under attack from a number of politically motivated groups.

Solicitors: Goodman Derrick & Co; Kingsley Napley & Co.

NOT YET THE TIMES

THE HAPIEST DAYS OF THERE LIFES

Swallowing Amazons

'Why are you and Peggy called the Amazons, Nancy?'

'Well, it certainly isn't because we've cut one breast off!' Nancy laughed merrily and continued to whittle her jibstay. 'Oh, I know *that*,' John said impatiently. 'Peggy showed me when you were caulking Captain Flint's bottom. She's the one who ought to be called Titty.'

'If it comes to that, why are you called the Swallows?' 'That was Susan's idea,' John admitted. 'It was after she saw some film that really impressed her – *Deep Boat* I think it was called.'

'Shiver my timbers! You're still a bit of a landlubber aren't you?' Nancy whacked John playfully with her jibstay. 'Look, let's pop into your tent and I'll show you what Susan really meant . . . .'

A scream rent the air. 'But, Nancy,' John stammered. 'You are . . . you are . . . a *boy*!' 'Of course I am. Why do you think I'm called Nancy, duckie?'

J. M. CROOKS

Christopher Robin Goes Coughety Cough

Christopher Robin is drawing his pension;
  He lives in a villa in Spain;
He suffers from chronic bronchitis and tension,
  And never goes out in the rain.

He never wears wellies; he has to eat jellies,
  He peers through a pair of bifocals;
He talks quite a lot to a bear that he's got
  Who is known as El Pu to the locals.

Christopher Robin goes coughety coughety
  Coughety coughety cough;
All sorts and conditions of Spanish physicians
  Have seen him and written him off.

But drowsily still in his house in Seville
He dreams of the Forest, and Anne,
Who waits in the buttercups – deep in the buttercups –
Down by the stream – for her man.

Little Known Last Moments

Mr Salteena

Dam and blarst said Mr Salteena flinging aside his wifes prayer book I shall go and see Ethel today. He cheerd up and put on his suit of velvit cote and green knickerbockers. He carefully rubbd the seat part with oderclone witch had gone shiny from horse galloping. He poked the doorbell of Ethels manshon with his riding crop. If this is sin I like it thought Mr Salteena. A maid showed him into a costly room with gay sofas. He helped himself to a large wiskey and took a fat sigar. A lovely vishon came it was Ethel. Mr Salteena sprang to his feet and said egerly I cannot stand sour grapes and ashes any longer come away with me. You filty beast gasped Ethel the wages of Sin is Deth. She took a little gun from a fringy evenig bag and shot him. Mr Salteena died.

P. M. ROBERTSON

William and the Gang Bang

'To the woods!' said William.
　'What for?' said Violet Elizabeth. 'Are you going to play with me?'
　'We're going to rape you,' said William. 'Aren't we, Ginger?'
　'Course,' said Ginger, dutifully.
　'What's wape?' lisped Violet Elizabeth.
　Clearly, William had aroused her interest.
　William hesitated. 'Well – er,' he said. 'Everyone knows what rape is, don't they, Ginger?'
　'Course,' replied Ginger. 'Everyone knows that.'
　He, William, wished he had been able to see what Robert and his latest girl-friend had actually been *doing* when he, William, watched

them through the window of his, Robert's car, parked in the drive the previous evening.

But Violet Elizabeth was having misgivings. 'I'll thcream and thcream till I'm thick,' she said. 'I *can*,' she added.

'How loud can you scream?' asked William.

Violet Elizabeth screamed, not very loudly.

'To the woods!' said William. 'C'mon, Ginger!'

* * * *

'Crumbs!' said William. 'She *has* been "thick".'

TOM LAWRENCE

You Are Old, Father William

A parody of Robert Southey's didactic poem 'The Old Man's Comforts and How He Gained Them':

> *'You are old, father William', the young man cried,*
> *'The few locks which are left you are grey;*
> *You are hale, father William, a hearty old man;*
> *Now tell me the reason, I pray.'*

> *'In the days of my youth,' father William replied,*
> *'I remember'd that youth would fly fast,*
> *And abus'd not my health and my vigour at first,*
> *That I never might need them at last.'*

'You are old, father William,' the young man said,
'And your hair has become very white;
And yet you incessantly stand on your head –
Do you think, at your age, it is right?'

'In my youth,' father William replied to his son,
'I feared it might injure the brain;
But, now that I'm perfectly sure I have none,
Why, I do it again and again.'

'You are old,' said the youth, 'as I mentioned before,
And have grown most uncommonly fat;
Yet you turned a back-somersault in at the door –
Pray what is the reason of that?'

'In my youth,' said the sage, as he shoot his grey locks,
   'I kept all my limbs very supple
By the use of this ointment – one shilling the box –
   Allow me to sell you a couple?'

'You are old,' said the youth, 'and your jaws are too weak
   For anything tougher than suet;
Yet you finished the goose, with the bones and the beak –
   Pray, how did you manage to do it?'

'In my youth,' said his father, 'I took to the law,
   And argued each case with my wife;
And the muscular strength, which it gave to my jaw,
   Has lasted the rest of my life.'

'You are old,' said the youth, 'one would hardly suppose
   That your eye was as steady as ever;
Yet you balanced an eel on the end of your nose –
   What made you so awfully clever?'

'I have answered three questions, and that is enough,'
   Said his father, 'Don't give yourself airs!
Do you think I can listen all day to such stuff?
   Be off, or I'll kick you down stairs!'

LEWIS CARROLL

Biggles Comes Through

The plane banked sharply to the left as we hurtled downwards, but the Fokker Wolf was still on our tail.

'A-a-a-a-a-a-a-zing,' went the twin cowl-mounted Mittelschmertz 25 mm cannons.

'Peng!' it went, in German, as one of the shells bit into the sleek wooden fuselage.

'Peng?' cogitated Biggles. 'That's the German for "Bang!"'

'We've been hit,' volunteered Ginger grimly.

'Nothing,' said Biggles grimlier, as he slipped his leather-gloved hand over the by now moistened joystick. He pulled it back in a series of sharp jerks.

'Level off a mo,' put in Algy drily and through drawn lips stepped purposefully into the body of the aircraft, past the by now shapely nude lady navigator; and back into the rear of the plane. The door of the Gents Only Sauna hung precariously from one hinge. He slammed it shut with a haunting squawk, and fought his way past the two naked WAFs wrestling in perfumed sump-oil. He erupted into the Aft Leather Room, to find Wingco still chained to a cross, wearing the by now familiar black hood bearing the also familiar Wing Commanderic braid.

'Have your way with me, you hunk of manhood,' he hinted coyly.

'What ho, old sport!' hazarded Algy gingerly. 'I say, old man, the Group's a bit dashed worried – thinks you might have some kind of, well . . . you know, problem . . . you old bison. . . .' He fingered his cigarette nervously.

'Don't worry about me, old tapir, I've pulled through a lot worse than this.'

The plane lurched suddenly as Biggles swerved to avoid a hail of bullets that pumped in spurts out of the penis-like nosecone of the pursuing Fokker. Algy rushed for'ard.

'Everything OK, Skipper?' he admitted.

'We haven't made it yet,' inserted Biggles, as he gritted his thighs and plunged his machine into a savage spin.

As they plunged downwards, the mighty engines throbbed and the well-lubricated pistons thrust themselves back and forth in their vice-like steel sheaths.

'You look a bit green around the gills, old eland,' observed Biggles smoothly.

'Never felt better,' puked Algy. . . .

GRAHAM CHAPMAN
A Liar's Autobiography

Another Cautionary Verse
[after Hilaire Belloc]

Paul Potter from an early age
Was moved by the poetic rage
And constantly amazed his nurses
By writing cautionary verses
Till Nanny Rose (who'd been to Girton –
St Hugh's – or Newnham – I'm not certain)
Said laughingly, 'My little man,
Your scansion's quite Edwardian;
You'll never reach the best Reviews
Unless you sound more like Ted Hughes.'
Paul screamed till he was sick; but No,
He couldn't take to eating *Crow;*
Guts left him cold; he was unable
To find life less than tolerable.
Instead he taught his feet to stray
By Ambler-side and Greene-away,
Wrote highbrow thrillers, made a splash
And gained a vast amount of cash.
The moral is: Ignore adverse
Criticism from your nurse.

FOXIE

Christmas Afternoon
[Dickens updated]

What an afternoon! Mr Gummidge said that, in his estimation, there
never had *been* such an afternoon since the world began, a sentiment
which was heartily endorsed by Mrs Gummidge and all the little Gum-
midges, not to mention the relatives who had come over from Jersey
for the day.

In the first place, there was the *ennui*. And such *ennui* as it was! A
heavy, overpowering *ennui*, such as results from a participation in eight
courses of steaming, gravied food, topping off with salted nuts which
the little old spinster Gummidge from Oak Hill said she never knew

when to stop eating – and true enough she didn't – a dragging, devitalising *ennui*, which left its victims strewn about the living room in various attitudes of prostration suggestive of those of the petrified occupants in a newly unearthed Pompeiian dwelling; an *ennui* which carried with it a retinue of yawns, snarls and thinly veiled insults, and which ended in ruptures in the clan spirit serious enough to last throughout the glad new year.

Then there were the toys! Three and a quarter dozen toys to be divided among seven children. Surely enough, you or I might say, to satisfy the little tots. But that would be because we didn't know the tots. In came Baby Lester Gummidge, Lillian's boy, dragging an electric grain-elevator which happened to be the only toy in the entire collection that appealed to little Norman, five-year-old son of Luther, who lived in Rahway. In came curly-headed Effie in frantic and throaty disputation with Arthur, Jr, over the possession of an articulated zebra. In came Everett, bearing a mechanical negro which would no longer dance, owing to a previous forcible feeding by the baby of a marshmallow into its only available aperture. In came Fonlansbee, teeth buried in the hand of little Ormond, who bore a popular but battered remnant of what had once been the proud false bosom of a hussar's uniform. In they all came, one after another, some crying, some snapping, some pulling, some pushing – all appealing to their respective parents for aid in their intramural warfare.

And the cigar smoke! Mrs Gummidge said that she didn't mind the smoke from a good cigarette, but would they mind if she opened the windows for just a minute in order to clear the room of the heavy aroma of used cigars? Mr Gummidge stoutly maintained that they were good cigars. His brother, George Gummidge, said that he, likewise, would say that they were. At which colloquial sally both Gummidge brothers laughed testily, thereby breaking the laughter record for the afternoon.

Aunt Libbie, who lived with George, remarked from the dark corner of the room that it seemed just like Sunday to her. An amendment was offered to this statement by the cousin, who was in the insurance business, stating that it was worse than Sunday. Murmurings indicative of as hearty agreement with this sentiment as their lethargy would allow came from the other members of the family circle, causing Mr Gummidge to suggest a walk in the air to settle their dinner.

And then arose such a chorus of protestations as has seldom been

141

heard. It was too cloudy to walk. It was too raw. It looked like snow. It looked like rain. Luther Gummidge said that he must be starting along home soon, anyway, bringing forth the acid query from Mrs Gummidge as to whether or not he was bored. Lillian said that she felt a cold coming on, and added that something they had had for dinner must have been under-cooked. And so it went, back and forth, forth and back, up and down, and in and out, until Mr Gummidge's suggestion of a walk in the air was reduced to a tattered impossibility and the entire company glowed with ill-feeling.

ROBERT BENCHLEY

Five Go Mad in Dorset

The children are seen cycling through the countryside. They stop on the brow of a hill overlooking rolling countryside and are having a picnic.

DICK. I say, this is a jolly wizard lunch, Anne. You're really going to make someone a great little wife one day.

JULIAN. Umm. My favourite. Ham and turkey sandwiches, heaps of tomatoes, fresh lettuce and lashings of ginger beer.

In the background two men, Rooky and Hunchy, are seen carrying a box across a field. They stop and start digging a pit.

ANNE. This is just the kind of holiday I like, picnicky meals and not too much adventure.

DICK. Well don't speak too soon, old thing.

A black car draws up. A black-gloved hand throws out a piece of meat.

MAN'S VOICE. Here, Fido.

He drives off at speed. Timmy, the dog, gobbles the meat.

GEORGE. That's strange. Why on earth would somebody want to feed Timmy?

JULIAN. Yes that was rather odd.

142

DICK. Ssh. I say look over there.

They notice the two men digging.

GEORGE. What a strange pair!

JULIAN. Yes one's got a big nose and thick lips and the other one's got mean, clever little eyes.

DICK. And they're unshaven. Just look how they're slouching.

ANNE. Urgh! Pooh! I hope they don't come near us. I feel as if I can smell them from here.

GEORGE. Ssh. I can hear them talking.

HUNCHY. What about the sparklers, Rooky?

ROOKY. Don't worry, Hunchy, I'll take care of that.

HUNCHY. Well now that you're out of gaol you'd better lie low.

GEORGE. D'you think they're escaped convicts?

DICK. Yes, or traitors to our country.

JULIAN. We'd better call the police.

ANNE. Oh look Timmy's fallen over.

Timmy is lying still in the grass.

GEORGE. Oh crikey, he's been poisoned!

JULIAN. Never mind, George, we'll get another. Come on everybody let's find a telephone!

They cycle off . . . .

PETER RICHARDSON AND PETER RICHENS
The Comic Strip Presents . . .

Poetic Licence

Remember Lot's Wife
after Kingsley Amis

Sometimes in later years
    dining with bosom pals
Lot felt a nervous wreck
    passing the salt.
But on the evidence
    (Genesis 19 *et seq.*)
Mrs Lot's tragic end
    wasn't his fault.

Poor sod was queer of course,
    shouldn't have married her,
Sex-starved and sore-eyed
    she looked back in tears.
Nothing but ashes and
    sodium chloride
Thank God I'm hetero,
    whisky please, cheers.

STANLEY J. SHARPLESS

Keeping Up With Kingsley
[after John Wain]

Ah well! It's good to be rid of all the strain.
It's such a pain to turn the drivel out.
(*And* to keep up with Kingsley and John Braine!)

Of course, they never saw what I was about:
Emancipation from the printed page . . . !
How's that for a way to still the doubter's doubt,
A slogan for the post-McLuhan age?

Poems should be read out loud. Mine too!

                              But man
You'd think they'd let you make a living wage

A *Word Carved on a Sill.* We do what we can.
OK, I was wrong to back the Empson horse:
I couldn't even get the stuff to scan;

Words never let you conquer them by force.
But certain possibilities remain.
I'll make a new anthology. And of course
I'll have to take up lecturing again.

COLIN FALCK

On Wordsworth

He lived amidst th' untrodden ways
    To Rydal Lake that lead;
A bard whom there was none to praise,
    And very few to read.

Behind a cloud his mystic sense,
    Deep hidden, who can spy?
Bright as the night when not a star
    Is shining in the sky.

Unread his works – his 'Milk White Doe'
    With dust is dark and dim;
It's still in Longman's shop, and oh!
    The difference to him!

HARTLEY COLERIDGE

148

The Higher Pantheism in a Nutshell
after Tennyson

One, who is not, we see; but one, whom we see not, is:
Surely this is not that: but that is assuredly this.

What, and wherefore, and whence? for under is over and under:
If thunder could be without lightning, lightning could be without
      thunder.

Doubt is faith in the main: but faith, on the whole, is doubt:
We cannot believe by proof: but could we believe without?

Why, and whither, and how? for barley and rye are not clover:
Neither are straight lines curves: yet over is under and over.

Two and two may be four: but four and four are not eight:
Fate and God may be twain: but God is the same thing as fate.

Ask a man what he thinks, and get from a man what he feels:
God, once caught in the fact, shows you a fair pair of heels.

Body and spirit are twins: God only knows which is which:
The soul squats down in the flesh, like a tinker drunk in a ditch.

More is the whole than a part: but half is more than the whole:
Clearly, the soul is the body: but is not the body the soul?

One and two are not one: but one and nothing is two:
Truth can hardly be false, if falsehood cannot be true.

Once the mastodon was; pterodactyls were common as cocks:
Then the mammoth was God: now is He a prize ox.

Parallels all things are: yet many of these are askew:
You are certainly I: but certainly I am not you.

Springs the rock from the plain, shoots the stream from the rock:
Cocks exist for the hen: but hens exist for the cock.

God, whom we see not, is: and God, who is not, we see:
Fiddle, we know, is diddle: and diddle, we take it, is dee.

ALGERNON CHARLES SWINBURNE

A Melton Mowbray Pork Pie

[after Swinburne]

Strange pie that is almost a passion,
    O passion immoral for pie!
Unknown are the ways that they fashion,
    Unknown and unseen of the eye.
The pie that is marbled and mottled,
    The pie that digests with a sigh;
For all is not Bass that is bottled
    And all is not pork that is pie.

RICHARD LE GALLIENNE

Betjeman, 1984

I saw him in the Airstrip Gardens
    (Fahrenheit at 451)
Feeding automative orchids
    With a little plastic bun,
While above his brickwork cranium
    Burned the trapped and troubled sun.

'Where is Piper? Where is Pontefract?
    (Devil take my boiling pate!)
Where is Pam? And where's Myfanwy?
    Don't remind me of the date!
Can it be that I am *really*
    Knocking on for 78?

'In my splendid State Apartment
    Underneath a secret lock
Finger now forbidden treasures
    (Pray for me St Enodoc!):
TV plate and concrete lamp-post
    And a single nylon sock.

150

'Take your ease, pale-haired admirer,
    As I, half the century saner,
Pour a vintage Mazawattee
    Through the Marks and Spencer strainer
In a *genuine* British Railways
    (Luton Made) cardboard container.

'Though they say my verse-compulsion
    Lacks an interstellar drive,
Reading, Beverley and Daphne
    Keeps *my* sense of words alive.
Lord, but *how* much beauty was there
    Back in 1955!'

CHARLES CAUSLEY

Book Review

Longest and much the dearest —
The price of books benumbs —
With a slap of sail and a following gale
The rhymer Causley comes.

Now Causley comes from Cornwall,
And, brother, how it shows.
The harbour bell and that fishy smell
Assault both ears and nose.

But Causley's balladeering
Is good for youth to gnaw on
(In fact, to be frank, it's a Doggerel Bank
That any kid can draw on).

He uses simply, sociably,
The skill he's been allotted;
And that's a start. Because in art
Not all the cream is clotted.

RUSSELL DAVIES

Ancient Music

Winter is icummen in,
Lhude sing Goddamm,
Raineth drop and staineth slop,
And how the wind doth ramm!
   Sing: Goddamm.
Skiddeth bus and sloppeth us,
An ague hath my ham.
Freezeth river, turneth liver,
   Damn you, sing: Goddamm.
Goddamm, Goddamm, 'tis why I am, Goddamm,
   So 'gainst the winter's balm.
Sing goddamm, damm, sing Goddamm,
Sing goddamm, sing goddamm, DAMM.

EZRA POUND

February Filldyke
[after Gerard Manley Hopkins]

Praiséd be God for February rain,
Fill dyke, flushmeadow, floatark, when from lower
Of skies stippled, dun-dappled, black-grey-hatched, shower
Cleanly descends on our oh in need of cleansing plain.
Restitution here repénts. Lént's the fit, fasting-fit, tear-washed reason
   of
Racing these level with, rival with its rim stream.
Root-mined tree's tumble, eddy-gashed clay's fall, is water's seisin of
Earth, earth's of water, in foam's yellow cream.
But *this,* my Moses, bank, *these* rushes rain-spent dawn to dark,
Wind-worried, flood-tugged into turbulent water,
No footing offer for a Pharaoh's fair daughter,
No haven, hid harbour, mooring for your pitched wattle ark.

R. J. P. HEWISON

Walk Whitman Retrospectively Addresses Old King Cole

Me clairvoyant,
Me conscious of you, old camarado,
Needing no telescope, lorgnette, field-glass, opera-glass, myopic
    pince-nez,
Me piercing two thousand years with eye naked and not ashamed;
The crown cannot hide you from me;
Musty old feudal-heraldic trappings cannot hide you from me,
I perceive that you drink.
(I am drinking with you. I am as drunk as you are.)
I see you are inhaling tobacco, puffing, smoking, spitting
(I do not object to your spitting),
You prophetic of American largeness,
You anticipating the broad masculine manners of these States;
I see in you also there are movements, tremors, tears, desires for the
    melodious,
I salute your three violinists, endlessly making vibrations,
Rigid, relentless, capable of going on for ever;
They play my accompaniment; but I shall take no notice of any
    accompaniment;
I myself am a complete orchestra.
So long.

                            G.K. CHESTERTON

Old King Cole
[after W. B. Yeats]

Of an old King in a story
    From the grey sea-folk I have heard,
Whose heart was no more broken
    Than the wings of a bird.

As soon as the moon was silver
    And the thin stars began,
He took his pipe and his tankard,
    Like an old peasant man.

153

And three tall shadows were with him
And came at his command;
And played before him for ever
The fiddles of fairyland.

And he died in the young summer
Of the world's desire;
Before our hearts were broken
Like sticks in a fire.

G. K. CHESTERTON

Chard Whitlow

Mr Eliot's Sunday Evening Postscript

As we get older we do not get any younger.
Seasons return, and today I am fifty-five,
And this time last year I was fifty-four,
And this time next year I shall be sixty-two.
And I cannot say I should like (to speak for myself)
To see my time over again – if you can call it time:
Fidgeting uneasily under a draughty stair,
Or counting sleepless nights in the crowded tube.

There are certain precautions – though none of them very reliable –
Against the blast from bombs and the flying splinter,
But not against the blast from heaven, *vento dei venti,*
The wind within a wind unable to speak for wind;
And the frigid burnings of purgatory will not be touched
By any emollient.
            I think you will find this put,
Better than I could ever hope to express it,
In the words of Kharma: 'It is, we believe,
Idle to hope that the simple stirrup-pump
Will extinguish hell.'
            Oh, listeners,
And you especially who have turned off the wireless,
And sit in Stoke or Basingstoke listening appreciatively to the silence,

(Which is also the silence of hell) pray, not for your skins, but your
    souls.

And pray for me also under the draughty stair.
As we get older we do not get any younger.
And pray for Kharma under the holy mountain.

HENRY REED

Rondel

Behold the works of William Morris,
    Epics, and here and there wall-papery,
    Mild, mooney, melancholy vapoury
A sort of Chaucer *minus* Horace.

Spun out like those of William Loris,
    Who wrote of amorous red-tapery,
Behold the works of William Morris,
    Epics, and here and there wall-papery!

Long ladies, knights, and earles and choris
    ters in the most appropriate drapery,
    Samite and silk and spotless napery,
Sunflowers and apple blossoms and orris,
Behold the works of William Morris!

ANON

A Country Fair
by Hernia Whittlebot
[after Edith Sitwell]

Chipperty, chap,
    Croperty, bibberty,
Snib, Snobb,
    Mop in wooh,
Clinter, clanter,
    Shinter, shanter,
Oggledy, boggledy, roops ahoo!

Danderley, Plockinsnitch,
Keedle-weedle, Keedle bim
Rift,
Toft,
Keek,
Snoop,
Piddery,
Frickaty,
Ramperty Toop.

Griberty grap
Voberty, Viberty,
Drib, Drob,
Yock in fooh,
Younter, Yanter,
Minter, Manter,
Nutlety, puttlety, Oggsie, Booh!

NOËL COWARD

The Man Who Hangs Head Downwards
[after Housman]

The man hangs head downwards
Against the shaking sky
Reflects me in the water
And who he is or why
He knows no more than I

I stir, he shifts beneath me
I halt, he stands stock still;
He knows not what constrains him
To move against his will
He only knows it ill.

And both will drown together
The mirrored man, and I
One falls, one rises upwards
To break the painted sky
But both of us will die.

KATHARINE WHITEHORN

After the Library
[after Philip Larkin]

After the library and tea (tired cakes in plastic wraps)
I pad the dappled park I once forsook.
The scented summer wind whirls dust and scraps
Against the thighs of mini-skirted girls,
Exposing nylon flimsies, lemon, rose;
Cheap thrills, you might suppose,
To one who, life half-gone, bends to a book.

But I was always easily bored, withdrawn:
The gilt-edged promises that life unfurls
Like paper flowers are flawed. A broken chime
Of fading laughter drifts up from the lawn.
Soon the dark-visaged keeper will call time.

DOUGLAS GIBSON

From the Spanish Cloister
[after Browning]

Grrr — what's that? A dog? A poet?
    Uttering his damnations thus —
If hate killed things, Brother Browning,
    God's Word, would not hate kill us?

If we ever meet together,
    Salve tibi! I might hear
How you know poor monks are really
    So much worse than they appear.

157

There's a great text in Corinthians
   Hinting that our faith entails
Something else, that never faileth,
   Yet in you, perhaps, it fails.

But if *plena gratia* chokes you,
   You at least can teach us how
To converse in wordless noises,
   Hy, zi; hullo!-Grrr – Bow-wow!

G. K. CHESTERTON

Squeal
[after Allen Ginsburg]

I saw the best minds of my generation
Destroyed – Marvin
Who spat out poems; Potzrebie,
Who coagulated a new bop literature in fifteen
Novels; Alvin
Who in his as yet unwritten autobiography
Gave Brooklyn an original *lex loci.*
They came from all over, from the pool room,
The bargain basement, the rod,
From Whitman, from Parkersburg, from Rimbaud
New Mexico, but mostly
They came from colleges, ejected
For drawing obscene diagrams of the Future.

They came here to LA,
Flexing their members, growing hair,
Planning immense unlimited poems,
More novels, more poems, more autobiographies.

It's love I'm talking about, you dirty bastards!
Love in the bushes, love in the freight car!
I saw them fornicating and being fornicated,
Saying to Hell with you!

America.
America is full of Babbitts.
America is run by money.
What was it Walt said? Go West!
But the important thing is the return ticket.
The road to publicity runs by Monterey.
I saw the best minds of my generation
Reading their poems to Vassar girls,
Being interviewed by *Mademoiselle*,
Having their publicity handled by professionals.
When can I go into an editorial office
And have my stuff published because I'm weird?
I could go on writing like this forever . . . .

LOUIS SIMPSON

After Walter de la Mare

Once upon a time. . . a time
   Again, encore, and anew,
Martha would tell us stories –
   Her eyes were blue.

Her eyes were deep as ocean
   You lave in, and her tales
Were beautiful, were beautiful,
   As bellied sails.

She'd speak, and her hind-white hands
   Would twine about her hocks,
While we hearkened, rapt, enthralled,
   And smelt the phlox.

Her voice was deep as ether
   Her dimpled chin was fine,
And she told lovely stories,
   In the sunshine.

159

'Once. . . once upon a time,'
   Martha, like the brook, trilled on;
Our hearts stood still with poring
   On times agone.

Times agone, and forgot . . .
   'But the stories she told?' you insist.
I dare not say, since Martha loved
   Freud, as I wist.

KENNETH SCOTT

Place Names of China
[after John Betjeman]

Bolding Vedas! Shanks New Nisa!
Trusty Lichfield swirls it down
To filter beds on Ruislip Marshes
From my loo in Kentish Town.

The Burlington! the Rochester!
Oh, those names of childhood loos;
Nursie knocking at the door –
'Have you done your number twos?'

Lady typist – office party –
Golly! all that gassy beer!
Tripping home down Hendon Parkway
To her Improved Windermere.

Chelsea buns and lounge bar pasties
All swilled down with Benskin's Pale;
Purified and cleansed with charcoal,
Fill the taps in Colindale.

Here I sit, alone and sixty;
Bald, and fat, and full of sin,
Cold the seat and loud the cistern,
As I read the Harpic tin.

ALAN BENNETT

Dear Father Christmas
[after Auden's 'Night Mail']

Dear Father Christmas, What are you bringing
Over the rooftops of Oxford winging?

Crackers for the mad, boaters for the Seine,
A drop of the hard stuff, a choo-choo train.

Zipping past Balliol, a shower of sparks
The porter's collie-dog, Prurient, barks.

Past coffee-bars and ancient tuckshops
Peeping through windows of red-lit brothels

'Look at Merton,' Santa hollers,
'Silent smiles of toil-bent scholars.'

Statues awaken as on he races,
Peep from niches at his Day-Glo braces.

A startled owl stops dead in its tracks
And gets knocked cold by the flying sacks.

In the Ashmolean, never a word
But on to the roof slops a reindeer turd.

ii
Dawn threatens. Is Santa done?
Down towards Reading he inclines
Towards the Third Division of the Football League
Towards the feel of Lux-lene curtains, the new settee,
Set on the foam-back like reclining hippos.
All Berkshire waits for him:
In Suburb, settee of the plain,
Men long for socks.

iii
Stockings of green, stockings obscene,
Stockings that smell and swell as well,
Abysmal stripe and ghastly tartan
Hairy calf-length, anklet spartan,
'Product of Italy', 'Made in Dumbarton',
Wrapped in a tissue, sealed in a carton,

' "Never without 'em," says E. Lustgarten,'
Hose enjoyable, hose unemployable,
Tights giving too much room for the kneecaps,
Tights fitted out with rude-looking pee-caps,
Tights for the winter, ballet and sex,
Tights where the spot is marked with an X,
Thick tights for journeyers, thicker for hernias,
Knitted in nylon of every shade,
The puce, the indigo, orange and jade,
The knotty, the spotty, the been-to-the menders,
The very-hard-wearing from Marks and Suspenders,
See-through, stay-fresh, tweed or twee,
The limp and the lumpy and the just-not-for-me.

iv
Millions are still abed
Dreaming of mollifying taxmen.
Or a friendly feel behind the shelves in stock-room or store-room.
Abed in working Reading, working in a well-read Oxford,
Reading in Welwyn Garden City,
They continue their snooze,
But shall wake soon and nudge their neighbour
And none will play at postman's knock
Without a heartening of the quick.
For who can bear to feel himself
At Christmas?

RUSSELL DAVIES

Anachronisms

Paradise Lost 0 - 1
[after Milton]

Their tumult ceased awhile, th'encircling throng,
Agape with keen anticipation, see,
Like coloured marbles roll'd on the green sward
By young Olympians, th'opposing Teams
Now scatter as the Contest starts, Flies now,
As if some insect were caught in the Game
The Gods play with mere men, a speckl'd sphere;
Nor does it come to rest in either net,
Though those who watch implore their several Gods
It should be; some one end, t'other some,
But wait awhile! When th'allotted Time's
Not half way done, Vict'ry attends one man:
Nor is't in vain! At last the argent Cup,
Spite foul attacks, is held up by his Chief.
Then, breaking loose, the herded hordes run free:
Relieve themselves, drink deep, and savage all
Who in their path might accident'ly stray.

MARGARET ROGERS

Brontë

Mr Botham is called to bowl. I avert my eyes to the scoreboard, yet
must be aware of that powerful presence. To my relief, he does not
look towards me; all his attention is for Mr Dyson, a dashing and
gentlemanlike figure at the far crease. Now I may gaze on Mr Botham
unobserved; with poignant, almost delicious agony, my eyes are drawn
to that strong nose and grim mouth whose power the reader knows I
have ever attempted to combat. He takes position, but hesitates. A
shadow, perhaps the memory of recent slights and sufferings, crosses his
features. I have no right to these turbulent thoughts, yet all of me,
blood, nerves, fibre and feelings gathers impulsively towards him as he

runs. The ball traverses the pitch, impelled by all the power of his splendid arrogant frame. Mr Dyson deflects it skilfully. Would that my poor soul could do as much!

GEORGE SIMMENS

The Fish Demon

Translator's note: Many must have wondered what is the relationship between fishermen and technicians on the Soviet trawlers which, loaded with electronic equipment, follow Nato exercises. As this recently discovered fragment shows, Russians have not changed. By a curious coincidence the hero of another Chekhov play, The Wood Demon, *which he later rewrote as* Uncle Vanya, *is called Krouschow.*

CAST:

ALEXANDER IVANOVICH NETSKY, a trawler captain

MARIA IVANOVNA NETSKY, his sister

ELENA ALEXANDROVNA NETSKY, his daughter

YEVGUENY PETROVICH MDEDIN, a ship's doctor

MASHA, his daughter

PIOTR, a young seaman, son of Netsky

SERGEI SONOVABICH RADARSKY, a naval captain

MIKHAIL BOFIN, a young electronics scientist.

ACT ONE

The after-deck of The People's Haddock, *a sturdy trawler of some 500 tons.* MASHA *is setting the table under an awning, while* PIOTR *watches her.*

PIOTR. Why do you wear black, Masha?

MASHA. Because it doesn't show the oil.

PIOTR. There's little enough fish oil here nowadays. If only we Russians ran our fishing-boats on rational principles! We ought to be knee-deep in turbot, mackerel, herring; iridescent, their scales flashing in the sun. You are so capable, Masha. You are not bored and fastidious like my sister Elena. Fish-oil stains would only give you a sweet dignity.

MASHA. It's not fish oil, it's engine oil. Sergei Sonovabich installed another hydraulic slewing mechanism today, controlled from the azication PPI.

PIOTR. What has happened to Russia? Today every intellectual talks glibly of time-base, thyratron jitter control, gate waveform. It's all dead, I tell you. But fish mean life, the *first* life, Masha! Come away with me! We will have our own fishing-boat, in the Baltic perhaps. Forget all this machinery! Let us find our true selves, not Nato. I love you, Masha.

MASHA. Fish! Ugh! How I hate them!

PIOTR. Then why do you stay here?

MASHA. Because I must. My father and yours would be helpless without me to cook and organise. Do you see that seagull? Sometimes I imagine I could fly away as freely as that to the Kiev Higher Technical Institute and learn more about radar, to help our Russia.

Enter ALEXANDER, MARIA, MDEDIN, RADARSKY, *all laughing.*

ALEXANDER. Just so, just so. We must move with the times, and all that. We have gone on too long in the old way in our Russian fisheries. Are you acquainted with the American author Hemingway? A pure soul! A great fisherman! Yes, tomorrow I shall take *The People's Haddock* to Cuba, to our Cuba. To the Caribbean, my friends! To the giant fish!

MARIA. Oh, I am so afraid! Unless we can make a great catch before next month our whole ship will be changed, given over to electronics. Our beautiful fish hold, our net store where I played as a little girl. Oh, the great sturgeon in the Black Sea, and songs of the fishermen, so passionate in the still evening! I think I am going to faint.

MDEDIN. Take some valerian drops. (*Humming:*) 'When I touched that fair cheek . . . .' Why, Masha, dear, what a feast! Anchovies, and Russian herrings!

PIOTR (*To* NETSKY). Yes, Father, it is a little surprise, a celebration. According to the log it is thirty-five years ago today that you became captain of *The People's Haddock*.

MARIA. Everything changes. I don't understand the young people. We did not have hydraulic nodding and slewing mechanisms in the Black Sea. Just the net store. And the fish holds. And the fishermen singing, all through the night.

RADARSKY. Dear lady, it is the only practical step. Do let me help you. It is no use whatever Alexander Ivanovich talking about the Caribbean. Only radar, and enemy signal jamming, can save your ship, and help our modern Russia.

MARIA. Yes, you are good and kind, Sergei Sonovabich. (*With a conscious effort at gaiety.*) Perhaps we can have fish *and* radar. A toast, everyone! Thirty-five years!

ALEXANDER. Thirty-five years! To the Caribbean! (*Swaying a little.*) The giant fish!

MDEDIN. Come, old chap, you must rest. I'll give you some valerian drops. (*Humming:*) 'Thy promises were in vain . . . .' (*Leads* ALEXANDER *off. The others, after a momentary silence, become convivial, except* PIOTR, *who suddenly rushes off after* MDEDIN.)

ACT TWO

The same. There is only one after-deck. ELENA, SERGEI *and* MASHA *are playing billiards.*

ELENA. I pot the white, I pot the red. Oh, how bored I am! What are fish? What is radar? I want to *live*. Yet no one understands.

Enter BOFIN.

SERGEI. This is Mihkail Bofin, our new electronics assistant.

MASHA (*eagerly*). Mikhail Grigorevich! We met on the refresher course at the Murmansk Polytechnic. Tell me, on the new set does the locking pulse go through the IF oscillator?

BOFIN *(briefly)*. Yes. *(To* ELENA.) Your eyes are like fire and ice. Will you do me the honour of looking round the new long-range equipment? (ELENA *goes out with him.*)

PIOTR. Masha, leave all this! Come with me, to the herring banks, to a free and beautiful life.

MASHA. Mikhail! Mikhail! Locking pulse! First in the class at Murmansk! Pure soul! Oh, how unhappy I am!

Bursts into tears. Curtain.

ACT THREE

The same, a month later. The awning has been taken down and the deck is stripped bare, and most of the deck planking has been taken up to make room for a large generator.

MARIA. Today is our last day on this beautiful ship, where I grew up. What is that hammering sound?

MASHA. They are taking down the last partition between No 2 and No 3 fish-holds, for the submarine range-finders. I pot the white, I pot the red, I pot the shrimp.

MARIA. Farewell the old life!

ALEXANDER. We shall never get to the Caribbean.

There is a silence but for the distant sounds of hammering. Then this, too, ceases. One single noise, which might be a hammer, or a shot, or an aerial mournfully, suddenly snapped. Enter MDEDIN.

MDEDIN. *(Humming:)* 'When I was young, in my father's boat . . . .' *(Aside to* ALEXANDER:) Get Masha away from here, anywhere. The fact is, Piotr has shot himself.

PAUL JENNINGS

Breakfast with Gerard Manley Hopkins

*'Delicious heart-of-the-corn, fresh-from-the-oven flakes are sparkled and
spangled with sugar for a can't-be-resisted flavour.'* Legend on a packet of
breakfast cereal.

Serious over my cereals I broke one breakfast my fast
   With something-to-read-searching retinas retained by print on a
      packet;
Sprung rhythm sprang, and I found (the mind fact-mining at last)
   An influence Father-Hopkins-fathered on the copy-writing racket.

Parenthesis-proud, bracket-bold, happiest with hyphens,
   The writers stagger intoxicated by terms, adjective-unsteadied,
Describing in graceless phrases fizzling like soda siphons
   All things crisp, crunchy, malted, tangy, sugared and shredded.

Far too, yes, too early we are urged to be purged, to savour
   Salt, malt and phosphates in English twisted and torn,
As, sparkled and spangled with sugar for a can't-be-resisted flavour,
   Come fresh-from-the-oven flakes direct from the heart of the corn.

ANTHONY BRODE

pūre~ly
ăcadĕm′ic

The Socratic Method

What is the argument of the Idealist School of Philosophy against the absolute existence, or externality, of the objects of experience? A question of this kind is best answered by the Socratic Method, an admirable arrangement whereby you call yourself 'Philosopher' and your opponent, who has no will of his own, 'Man In The Street' or 'Thrasymachus'. The argument then proceeds thus:

PHILOSOPHER. You will, I suppose, agree that the Understanding, through the same operations whereby in conceptions, by means of analytical unity, it produced the logical form of a judgment, introduces, by means of the synthetical unity of the manifold in intuition, a transcendental content into its representations, on which account they are called pure conceptions of the understanding?

THRASYMACHUS. Yes, I agree.

PHILOSOPHER. And further, is it not true that the mind fails in some cases to distinguish between actual and merely *potential* existence?

THRASYMACHUS. It is true.

PHILOSOPHER. Then S is P must be true of all predicative judgments?

THRASYMACHUS. Certainly.

PHILOSOPHER. And A is not not – A?

THRASYMACHUS. It is not.

PHILOSOPHER. So that every judgment may be taken either *intensively* or *extensively?*

THRASYMACHUS. Indubitably.

PHILOSOPHER. And this is through the activity of the apperceptive unity of self-consciousness, sometimes called cognition?

THRASYMACHUS. Indisputably.

PHILOSOPHER. Which arranges the phenomena of the sense-manifold in accordance with the principles of a primitive synthesis?

THRASYMACHUS. Incontrovertibly.

PHILOSOPHER. And these principles are the Categories?

THRASYMACHUS. Yeah!

PHILOSOPHER. Thus the universal is real and self-existent, and the particular only a quality of the understanding. So in the end your opinion is found to coincide with mine, and we agree that there is no *a priori* necessity for the continued existence of unperceived phenomena?

THRASYMACHUS. No. My opinion is that you are talking a lot of balderdash and ought to be locked up. Am I not right?

PHILOSOPHER. I suppose you are.

It will be observed that the Socratic Method is not infallible, especially when dealing with Thrasymachus.

H.F. ELLIS
So This is Science

How Your Body Works
by A. Nother Doctor

The human body is indeed a wonderful thing. Its infinitely complex way of functioning would take a computer, working flat out, day and night, excluding Bank Holidays and Christmas, 3,971 years to work out. The slightest flicker of the eyelid, the smallest movement of the big toe, involves such extraordinarily complex processes that the average man, working flat out, excluding Bank Holidays and Christmas, but *including* weekends, would take 84,643 light years to work it out. If you can imagine an Airedale terrier jumping in and out of a watering can once every 7 minutes for 12 years you have some idea how long that would take. And that's only one light year.

Even the most simple process that the body can perform – like paying the doctor – would take a piece of asbestos over 9 billion years to work out. If you can imagine a man at a cocktail party congratulating the hostess on the avocado dip 40,000 times every second for 2½ hours twice a week for 28,000 years you can begin to realise what an extraordinarily wonderful thing the human body is.

To put it even more simply, if you can imagine a doctor leaving his lucrative Harley St practice to a younger partner, and cruising round the world 4 times a year, drinking 3 bottles of champagne with a friend's wife every afternoon, and writing an article on How Your Body Works once every 96 days, you'll get some idea of why I was struck off the register. Good evening.

MONTY PYTHON
Monty Python's Big Red Book

Doing Snogging

Author's Note: 'Snogging' is British juvenile argot for low-profile, high-intensity, dyadic interaction. The research of which this paper is a part was supported by Air Force grant no. 999S.

The central recommendation of the following is that the proper brief of sociological enquiry is not the arid systematics of formalistic neo-Parsonian positivism, in which that-which-should-be-the-proper-brief-of-sociological-enquiry is taken-for-granted; but, rather that snogging – far from being the monolithic, role-specific, cultural reification that sociologists of the past three generations have taken as an unreflexive cultural residium of life-as-usual – is an ongoing, artful, negotiation of nonspecific role eruptions.[1] This emergent choreography à deux which is commended as the hitherto ignored accomplishment of everyday actors is precisely what this short paper sets itself the task of examining.

Critique Of Theory To Date
The reigning orthodoxy in sociological theory has for too long stood on the shoulders of giant glosses and has taken-as-given such artfully lustful extrusive interpersonal strivings as epiphenomenal to the sociology of the family. Only recently has it become possible[2] to stand this orthodoxy on its head in order to better view its privates.[3] The result of this orthodox leviathan's bullying of sociological data has been the sedimentation in the professional and everyday lexicon of words and phrases that attempt to hide the monster's true identity under the skirts of colloquies and thus skew the whole sociological enterprise from the outset by tainting the very words in our mouths.[4]

Hence, such unreflexive, common-sense, terminological polarities, wrapped in the guise of scientific sociology, as snogger/snoggee. What more proof is required that a hundred years of sociology has mistaken the explanans for the explanandum?[5]

Method Of Research

The aid of graduate students was enlisted to test the basic theoretical infrastructure of the problematic, as well as a long-standing professional curiosity of the author and some of his similarly inclined colleagues, to wit, generations of uncritical ingestion of orthodox sociological positivism has lent – on the social construction of reality thesis – a verisimilitude to everyday lexical items that – unsubstantiated in roles – gives them a veneer of veracity that – on the surface – supports the formalistic assertions of 'normal' sociology.[6] In other words, for the reasons that we have outlined and critically disposed of above, orthodox sociological theory appears, to the unreflexive sociologist, to be true.[7]

Example Of a Protocol

With the aid of the research grant already mentioned, it was possible to assemble video tape equipment, a parking lot, some cars and several enquiring graduate students. Following is an abbreviated excerpt of just one session in which the poverty of the accepted orthodox position was demonstrated.

Snogger = XY
Snoggee = XX

XY, 1.111. Humm!
XX, 1.111. Eh?
XY, 1.112. Com'ere!
XX, 1.112. Whats'at?
XY, 1.121. Here?
XX, 1.221. Whoocit!
(Clunk, Rustle.)
XY, 1.121. Careful!
XY, 1.221. Ha!
XX, 2.111. Hey!
(Scrape, Clank.)
XX, 2.112. Theresomekinkout'erwithacamera.

176

Conclusion

The shortfall of functional imperativistic sociological theory's ability to comprehend the emergent meaning of this ongoingly negotiated piece of social interaction becomes obvious in a 1::1 correlation with the apparent – but as far as the deep structure of the interaction is concerned, spurious – normalcy of the unfolding dramaturgical throughput. In other words, there was more to this brief interaction than would be visible to the 'normal' reader of most of our *acceptable* sociological journals.

The conclusion of such preliminary research is to us as profound as it is simple. A thoroughgoing and complete[8] revolution is called for in our approach to so-called sociological problems. A mere ninety degree turn left or right[9] would be no more than a quarter of the reorientation that is our central recommendation. A little more or less than this would merely render the questions more obtuse and their solution more acute, respectively. The time for comforting tautologies is past. Tomorrow's sociology will turn full cycle from the orthodoxy of today – it will be revolutionary sociology!

NOTES

1. See Karl Glotz, 'Ethnoepidemiology and the Negotiation of Sexuality on a Rural Californian Campus' (unpublished).
2. See N. Howe, 1. Publish, 'Excerpts from Students' Unpublished Ph.D. Theses' in Proceedings of the 5th Congress of the Mutual and Miration Society.
3. My neologism for the unreflexive axiological base and taken-for-granteds of a theoretical body.
4. See B. Pedodontis, 'A Reflexive Reexamination of Sociology's Oral Tradition' in Strict Training Practices of Victorian Sociologists.
5. Collins Pocket Latin Dictionary, p. 52.
6. By 'normal' sociology, I mean the pre-paradigm variety which, when compared to the history of theoretical revolutions, belies its claim to the status of a paradigm. (See Gad Flyburg, 'Introduction to Critical and Relaxed Sociological Theory'.)
7. George Flex (ed.) *Exercises for Reflexive Sociologists.*
8. 360 degrees.
9. A phenomenologically grounded sociology has no political axes to grind.

ROSS McLEOD

177

The Duchess of Wapping

Madcap Moll

Nobody who knew George I could help loving him – he possessed that peculiar charm of manner which had the effect of subjugating all who came near him into immediate slavery. Madcap Moll – his true love, his one love (England still resounds with her gay laugh) – adored him with such devotion as falls to the lot of few men, be they kings or beggars. They met first in the New Forest . . . .

Upon seeing him, Madcap Moll gave a merry laugh, and crying 'Chase me, George!' in provocative tones, she rode swiftly away on her pony. Many of the courtiers trembled at such a daring exhibition of *lèse majesté,* but the King, provoked only by her winning smile, tossed his gun to Lord Twirp and set off in hot pursuit. Eventually he caught his roguish quarry by the banks of a sunlit pool. She had flung herself off her mount and flung herself on the trunk of a tree, which she bestrode as though it were a better and more fiery steed. The King cast an appraising glance at her shapely legs, and then tethered his horse to an old oak.

'Are you a creature of the woods?' he said.

Madcap Moll tossed her curls. 'Ask me!' she cried derisively.

'I am asking you,' replied the King.

'Odds fudge – you have spindleshanks!' cried Madcap Moll irrelevantly. The King was charmed. He leant towards her.

'One kiss, mistress!' he implored. At that she slapped his face and made his nose bleed. He was captivated . . . .

NOËL COWARD
A Withered Nosegay

Il Minnestrone

Peasant Love

Scene: Venice and Old Point Comfort. Time: Early 16th century

CAST:

ALFONSO, Duke of Minnestrone   Baritone

PARTOLA, a Peasant Girl   Soprano

CLEANSO, Young nobleman of Venice   Tenor

TURINO, Young nobleman of Venice   Tenor

BOMBO, Young nobleman of Venice   Basso

LUDOVICVO, Assassin in the Service of Cafeteria Rusticana   Basso

ASTOLFO, Assassin in the Service of Cafeteria Rusticana   Methodist

TOWNSPEOPLE, CABBIES and SPARROWS

Argument
'Il Minnestrone' is an allegory of the two sides of a man's nature
(good and bad), ending at last in an awfully comical form with
everyone dead.

ACT 1
A Public Square, Ferrara. During a peasant festival held to celebrate
the sixth consecutive day of rain, RUDOLPHO a young nobleman,
sees LILLIANO, daughter of the village bell-ringer, dancing along
throwing artificial flowers at herself. He asks of his secretary who
the young woman is, and his secretary, in order to confuse
RUDOLPHO and thereby win the hand of his ward, tells him that it
is his (RUDOLPHO'S) own mother, disguised for the festival.
RUDOLPHO is astounded. He orders her arrest.

ACT 2
Banquet Hall in Gorgio's Palace. LILLIANO has not forgotten BREDA,
her old nurse, in spite of her troubles, and determines to avenge herself
for the many insults she received in her youth by poisoning her
(BREDA). She therefore invites the old nurse to a banquet and poisons
her. Presently a knock is heard. It is UGOLFO. He has come to carry
away the body of MICHAEL and to leave an extra quart of pasteurised.
LILLIANO tells him that she no longer loves him, at which he goes
away, dragging his feet sulkily.

179

ACT 3

In Front of Emilio's House. Still thinking of the old man's curse, BORSA has an interview with CLEANSO believing him to be the DUKE'S wife. He tells him things can't go on as they are, and CLEANSO stabs him. Just at this moment BETTY comes rushing in from school and falls in a faint. Her worst fears have been realised. She has been insulted by SIGMUNDO and presently dies of old age, in a fury. UGOLFO rushes out to kill SIGMUNDO and, as he does so, the dying ROSENBLATT rises on one elbow and curses his mother.

ROBERT BENCHLEY

O Felix Culpa!

The Sacramental Meaning of Winnie-the-Pooh

BY C.J.L. CULPEPPER, D. Litt, Oxon

C[YRUS] J[ACKSON] L[EE] CULPEPPER *was born in Baton Rouge and educated at Chapel Hill and Oxford. Although he is presently teaching at Southern Methodist, he wants your editor to assure his readers that he is 'not of the Dissenting persuasion'. He has published significant articles on the* Essay on Man, *Wordsworth's* White Doe of Rylestone, *and the works of Ivy Compton-Burnett, 'placing them all,' as he says, 'within the roomy fabric of the Christian-Humanist tradition.' Presently he is at work on a monograph proving that Shakespeare was familiar with the teachings of the Essene Sect and that his plays must be reinterpreted accordingly.*

Searching for a literary Saviour is, if I may confide in the reader, often a rather trying affair, since this personage must be an epitome of meekness and at the same time act as a strong moral guide for the other characters. In *Pooh* we have no dearth of meek characters, but a frustrating want of moral pronouncements. Yet there is one Character, blessedly, Who outdoes all the others in humility while managing, at one dramatic moment, to reveal His true identity in a divine Uttering: 'A little Consideration,' He says, 'a little Thought for Others, makes all the difference.' What an electrifying effect this produces on the reader!

180

At one stroke we have been transported back across all the materialistic heresies of the modern world, back safely across the wicked Counter-Reformation into the purity of Cranmer, Henry the Eighth, the early Church, and the Sermon on the Mount. Here we have none of the hypocrisy of the crafty Loyola, none of the foaming frenzy of the Anabaptists, but a simple assertion of the Golden Rule. The Speaker is of course Eeyore, the Lowly One, the Despised, Acquainted with Grief. His dictum of pure *caritas* is the moral standard by which every action of the lesser characters in *Winnie-the-Pooh* must be severely judged.

Once Eeyore's role has been understood, the reader will naturally be able to perceive innumerable familiar stages in His career. The chapter 'Eeyore Has a Birthday' is a charming parallel to the coming of the Magi, with Piglet and Pooh's balloon and pot forming a primitive but nonetheless heartfelt equivalent to frankincense and myrrh. The third gift of gold is supplied by Christopher Robin's generous offer of a box of paints. Eeyore's sermon against washing, 'this modern Behind-the-ears nonsense,' is His plea that we become as little children, avoiding, by the way, a confusion of materialistic porcelain-and-chrome 'progress' with genuine spiritual improvement. 'Take no thought for the morrow' would be an approximate rendering of His remark. Again, His placing of His tail in the stream when Roo appears to be drowning is His offer of salvation to all; Milne luckily realised the universal implications of the scene and resisted the opportunity to narrow them down by having only Roo, or indeed anyone, accept the offer. The giving of His own breakfast of thistles to Tigger reminds us of the Loaves and Fishes, but at the same time, to judge from Tigger's reaction, serves as a reminder that the path to Heaven is thorny. His breaking of Tigger's near-fatal *fall from a tree* (italics mine) is, in contrast, a very *exemplum* of the Atonement, while His later contemplation of three sticks forming the letter 'A' is an icon at once of the Trinity, the three Cardinal Virtues, and His Own role as the second Adam. His Baptism takes place in the Poohsticks chapter; His Last Supper is the farewell banquet in which He makes the central speech; His exchanging of an earthly home for a Heavenly one occurs in the 'Pooh Builds a House' episode; while His Own opening of the gates of the New Jerusalem for all the Saved is bodied forth in 'Eeyore Finds the Wolery'. Even His Name, as is invariably true in allegorical literature, contains a secret clue to His prototype. A phonetic transliteration into Italian (the language of sweet Boccaccio) yields us IO RE, 'I [Am the]

181

King.' That the King should be identified with the lowly Ass is a paradox which every reader of Scripture will recognise as quintessentially Christian . . . .

FREDERICK CREWS
The Pooh Perplex

History of England
Test Paper 1

Up to the end of 1066

1. Which do you consider were the more alike, Caesar or Pompey, or *vice versa*? (Be brief.)

2. Discuss, in latin or gothic *(but not both)*, whether the Northumbrian Bishops were more schismatical than the Cumbrian Abbots. (Be bright.)

3. Which came first, AD or BC ? (Be careful.)

4. Has it never occurred to you that the Romans *counted backwards?* (Be honest.)

5. How angry would you be if it was suggested
(1) That the XIth Chap. of the *Consolations of Boethius* was an interpolated palimpsest?
(2) That an eisteddfod was an agricultural implement?

6. How would you have attempted to deal with
(a) The Venomous Bead?
(b) A Mabinogion or Wapentake? (Be quick.)

7. What would have happened if *(a)* Boadicea had been the daughter of Edward the Confessor? *(b)* Canute had succeeded in sitting on the waves?

Does it matter?

8. Have you the faintest recollection of
(1) Ethelbreth?
(2) Athelthral?
(3) Thruthelthrolth?

9. What *have* you the faintest recollection of?

10. Estimate the average age of

(1) The Ancient Britons.

(2) Ealdormen.

(3) Old King Cole.

11. Why do you know nothing at all about

(a) The Laws of Infangthief and Egg-seisin?

(b) Saint Pancras?

12. Would you say that Ethelread the Unready was directly responsible for the French Revolution? If so, what *would* you say?

NB. *Do not attempt to answer more than one question at a time.*

W. C SELLAR AND R. J. YEATMAN
1066 and All That

THE BIG
SCREEN
SEEN

Balham – Gateway to the South

PETER. Balham – Gateway to the South!

Music.

PETER. We enter Balham through the verdant grasslands of Battersea Park and at once we are aware that here is a land of happy contented people who go about their tasks in truly democratic spirit.

Music.

PETER. This is busy High Street, focal point of the Town's activities. Note the quaint old stores whose frontage is covered with hand-painted inscriptions, every one a rare example of native Balham art. Let us read some of them as our camera travels past.

HARRY. Cooking apples – choice eaters – green ration books only.

MICHAEL. A Song to Remember at the Tantamount Cinema –

BENNY LEE. A Suit to Remember at Montague Moss.

BENNY HILL. Cremations Conducted With Decorum and Taste.

MICHAEL. Frying tonight. Bring your own paper.

HARRY. Rally Thursday. Berkeley Square – Bev Baxter and Quinny Hogg – Up the ruling classes.

PETER. This shows the manifold activities of Balham's thriving community. Yet Balham is also the home of a craftmanship which is slowly dying amid the industrialisation of the modern world, and in quiet corners we still find examples of the exquisite workmanship that Balham craftsmen have made world famous.

HARRY. Toothbrush holesmanship.

BENNY HILL. On my forge I carve these little holes in the top of toothbrushes. It is exciting work, and my forefathers have been engaged on it since 1957.

187

MICHAEL. I am a hair-pin corrugator. The bent bits in the middle of a hairpin – or, as we say in the trade, hairpin bends – are put in manually, or, in other words, once a year. I recently had the honour of demonstrating my craft before the Oni of Ife. He stopped by one day for a couple of words. I did not understand either of them.

PETER. Needless to say many of Balham's craftsmen today are engaged upon work which brings in much-needed dollars. An example is manufacture of spelkin binders. This is a fascinating process, a secret that is handed down from father to son.

MICHAEL. My boy, I'm going to hand it down to you. Guard it carefully. It is a priceless heritage. Here – take it.

Sound of crash.

MICHAEL. Butterfingers!

HARRY. Let us watch the last stages in the process of the manufacture of a typical spelkin binder in Balham's model factory.

BENNY HILL *(Australian)*. I am the factory manager. The boiling lead has just been poured from the graving crucible into a well-greased pan. The rubber slats are buckled in two at a time . . . .

Sound of slats being buckled in.

BENNY HILL. Next the galvanators . . . .

Sound of galvanators.

BENNY HILL. Followed by the trumble casing . . . .

Sound of trumble casing.

BENNY HILL. . . . and the meshed articulators. Next comes the prime grafter gudgeon pin . . .

Sound of gudgeon pin.

BENNY HILL. . . . then the doofah . . .

Sound of doofah.

BENNY HILL.... then the watchamacallit ....

Sound of watchamacallit.

BENNY HILL.... and the thingummybob ....

Sound of thingummybob.

BENNY HILL.... then that queer thing ....

Sound of queer thing.

BENNY HILL.... and the er ... howd'yedo ....

Sound of howd'yedo.

BENNY *(surprised)*.... then the – oh it's all over!

HARRY. The completed assembly is wheeled into the paint shop for a coat of green enamel from whence it is taken on huge lorries to all parts of the world where it will find its way on to the breakfast table of a million homes.

PETER. So much for Balham's industries. Let us see a little more of the town. Here is the Great Park, covering nearly half an acre.

Music.

PETER. This is where the children traditionally meet by the limpid waters of the old drinking fountain, a drinking fountain that has for countless years, across the vast aeons of time, given untold pleasure to man, woman and child – all three of them. Beside this fountain – donated by able Councillor Stephen Colgate as long ago as 1928 – the little ones sit round a trim nursemaid and listen spellbound and enchanted as she reads them a story.

PAT. With one bound he was by her side. She felt his hot breath on her cheek as he ripped the thin silk from –

Music.

189

PETER. We are now entering Old Balham. Time has passed by this remote corner. So shall we. But first let us take a peep at the inhabitants who carry about them the aura of a bygone era. This is Mrs Brisket, who as she chats to her neighbour still wears the colourful costume of long ago.

CAROLE. I said to my daughter, hem line or no hem line this skirt cost me six coupons and it's good enough for knocking about the house in.

PETER. But Balham does not live in the past, it looks to the future.

MICHAEL. Of course, the figures aren't available at the moment but the Housing Committee are considering plans for a new station waiting room and a crèche.

BENNY HILL. Councillor Colgate, my paper wants to know – what exactly is a crèche?

MICHAEL. Well, it's a – let's examine housing. By cutting red tape to the minimum we have housed *(cough)* families, requisitioned *(cough)* buildings and hope by the end of 1949 to have completed a further *(cough)*.

PETER. But Balham is not neglecting the cultural side. Balham has more bookshops and art museums than any other borough of the same name. This is Eugene Colgate whose weekly recitals are attended by a vast concord of people. He has never had a lesson in his life.

Piano played very badly.

PETER. Such is the enthusiasm of Balham's music lovers that they are subscribing to send Eugene to Italy. Or Vienna. Or anywhere. Paintings are on view in the Great Park during the summer and all the town's younger folk flock there in the evening for those primitive exhibitions.

Music.

PETER. Night falls on Balham.

Music.

190

PETER. From Colgate's Folly, Balham's famous beauty spot, which stands nearly two feet above sea level, the town is spread below us in a fairyland of glittering lights, changing all the time. Green, amber, red, red and amber, and back to green. The nightlife is awakening.

Music.

PETER. The El Morocco Tea Rooms.

HARRY. Hey, miss.

PAT. Yes? Watcha want?

HARRY. Pilchards.

PAT. They're off.

HARRY. Ah! Baked beans?

PAT. Off.

HARRY. Meat loaf salad?

PAT. Off.

HARRY. Pot of tea?

PAT. No tea.

HARRY. Well, just milk.

PAT. Milk's off.

HARRY. A roll and butter, then.

PAT. No butter.

HARRY. Just a roll.

PAT. Only bread.

HARRY. I might just as well've stayed at 'ome.

PAT. Ooh – I dunno – does you good to 'ave a fling occasionally.

Music.

PETER. And so the long night draws on. The last stragglers make their way home and the lights go out one by one as dawn approaches and the bell of St Colgate's parish church tolls ten o'clock. Balham sleeps, and so we say farewell to the historic borough with many pleasant memories and the words of G. Colgate Smith, Balham's own bard, burning in our ears.

MICHAEL.
> Broadbosomed, bold, becalm'd, benign
> Lies Balham foursquare on the Northern Line.
> Matched by no marvel save in Eastern scene,
> A rose-red city half as gold as green.
> By country churchyard, ferny fen and mere
> What Colgate mute, inglorious, lies buried here.
> Oh stands the church clock at ten to three
> And is there honey still for tea?

PAT. Honey's off.

Music.

PETER SELLERS

Aftermyth of War

ALAN. I had a pretty quiet war really. I was one of the Few. We were stationed down at Biggin Hill. One Sunday we got word Jerry was coming in, over Broadstairs, I think it was. We got up there as quickly as we could and you know, everything was very calm and peaceful. England lay like a green carpet below us, and the war seemed worlds away. I could see Tunbridge Wells and the sun glinting on the river, and I remembered that last weekend I spent there with Celia that summer of '39.

Suddenly, Jerry was coming at me out of a bank of cloud. I let him have it, and I think I must have got him in the wing because he spiralled past me out of control. As he did so, I will always remember this, I got a glimpse of his face, and you know, he *smiled*. Funny thing – war.

(Sound of hearty singing.)

(Enter PETER *on rostrum.)*

PETER. Perkins! Sorry to drag you away from the fun, old boy. War's
not going very well, you know.

JON. Oh my God!

PETER. We are two down, and the ball's in the enemy court. War is a
psychological thing, Perkins, rather like a game of football. And
you know how in a game of football ten men often play better than
eleven –?

JON. Yes, sir.

PETER. Perkins, we are asking you to be that one man. I want you to
lay down your life, Perkins. We need a futile gesture at this stage. It
will raise the whole tone of the war. Get up in a crate, over to
Bremen, take a shufti, don't come back. Goodbye, Perkins, God, I
wish I was going too.

JON. Goodbye, sir – or perhaps it's 'au revoir'?

PETER. No, Perkins.

Exit JON.

ALAN BENNETT, PETER COOK, JONATHAN MILLER and
DUDLEY MOORE
Beyond the Fringe

The Little Hut of Enmity

*[The characters in this 'Play for Yesterday' are Justin, an English stockbroker,
his wife Elspeth; Old Kurt and Young Kurt, Swiss mountain guides; Ilse, a
tall, blonde Aryan; and the Americans Mike and Maisie. Young Kurt is lost in
the snow; the others are sheltering from a blizzard in a remote mountain hut.]*

JUSTIN. Steady, old girl. Let's face the truth for the first time in our
lives. If I don't come back, all I ask is this, not that I have any right
to ask anything of you. Remember me as I am now; not that hollow
sham you lived with all those years, but a man doing, for the first

time in his life, the decent thing. Remember me as I am when I go through that door.

He steps to the door.

I may be some time.

He opens the door. The blizzard howls in. He makes a superhuman effort, trying to force himself into the wind.

The wind, it's too . . . I can't . . .

With a cry he collapses back, sobbing with frustration. The door slams shut.

I can't deal with the wind! Oh, God I'm too weak! Too weak!

ELSPETH. Oh, Justin, I do love you: do, do, love you . . . .

JUSTIN. I'm weak, weak . . . .

ELSPETH. No, Justin, you're strong, strong. Strong enough to know that you are weak. That is the greatest strength of all.

JUSTIN. Look after me, Elspeth. Take care of me. Don't leave me.

ELSPETH. There, there, my darling, there, there . . . .

JUSTIN. Mike, old man – I'm sorry . . . .

MIKE. I know, it's up to me now. It's ironical, isn't it? Suddenly I've got something to live for.

He gives an ironical laugh.

MAISIE. It takes a few old mountains to teach us the truth about ourselves. And somehow, when we face up to the truth, it stops being important any more.

ELSPETH. It's these mountains. They're wiser than any of us.

MIKE. I'll go then. I'll make it. I'm stronger than you. Justin, I've kept myself fit all these years, trained my body hard, tried to make a he-man of myself, to please my old dad. Ha! While deep down underneath –

MAISIE. Don't say it, Mike.

194

MIKE. Shut up, Maisie. You gotta know this before I – go out there. You gotta know who I really am, what I really am. You gotta know what I've been covering up all these years, when I was putting on the big all-American boy act . . . .

JUSTIN. If you mean your CIA work, I know about that . . . .

MIKE. Worse than that. Ah. Maisie, if only I'd met you ten years ago, you might have done something for me. Now it's too late.

MAISIE. It's never too late –

MIKE. Don't you understand what I'm telling you? That I'm rotten? A hollow sham? Well, I'll spell it out. Maisie, I'm queer! I'm a fruit, Maisie.

He sobs brokenly.

MAISIE. Why, you fool! Do you think I didn't know?

MIKE. You – knew?

MAISIE. Don't you understand, it makes no difference! I love you, Mike. Listen, we'll fight this thing, fight it together. And we'll win, Mike, we'll win. And now, go out there and find young Kurt. I'll be waiting for you. I love you. More than that. I – admire you, Mike.

MIKE. Shut up Maisie . . . . Well, I'll be seeing you.

He opens the door. Blizzard.

ILSE. No! You shall not go!

She shuts the door.

MIKE. Out of the way, Ilse! I gotta go!

ILSE. Stand back, I varn you!

She takes out a knife.

ELSPETH. Look out, she's got a knife! Keep away from her, Justin! She's mad!

JUSTIN. Give me that knife, Ilse. I said, give – me – that – knife!

ILSE. Keep beck, Englishman.

She stares at him, fighting him with her eyes and at the same time fighting within herself. She gives a broken, twisted smile.

So, I vas wrong. Wrong about you all. I took you to be veak, effete, despicable. Ach! I see now! All my life I have lived a lie. But I am not beaten yet. I go now. I shall prove that I, Ilse von Bahrendorfer, have still some Charman blood in my veins. Goodbye!

She opens the door. JUSTIN *grabs her.*

JUSTIN. No you don't!

ELSPETH. Look out, Justin!

ILSE. Let me go! I must prove myself!

They struggle. JUSTIN *gives a cry of pain.*

ELSPETH. Justin, you're hurt! Take that, you cow!

She hits ILSE *with her discarded snowboot.* ILSE *cries out and falls.*

JUSTIN. Well done, Elspeth; that snowboot came in handy.

ELSPETH. Justin, you're bleeding.

JUSTIN. Just a scratch.

MAISIE. My God, Ilse. She's fallen on the knife. Horrible, horrible . . . .

OLD KURT *gives a cry and begins to speak rapidly.*

MIKE. What's he saying? Ilse, for God's sake, what's the old man saying??

ILSE *(struggling to speak).* He say . . . zat ze avalanche . . . is coming. So . . . *(She gives a crooked laugh.)* Who vins . . . in ze end . . . and who . . . loses? *(She feebly raises one arm in salute.)* Heil –!

196

With a cry ILSE *passes out. The avalanche begins to be heard.* OLD KURT *takes charge of the situation, giving the others orders which they obey as best they can.*

JUSTIN. Listen. It's coming.

ELSPETH. It's strange, Justin. I feel oddly calm. I'm not frightened any more. It's as if it all happened long, long ago, in some far distant place to somebody else . . . .

JUSTIN. We've done the best we can. We've all done the best we can.

MAISIE. May God forgive us all.

MIKE. Shut up, Maisie.

JUSTIN. Here it comes . . . .

JAMES SAUNDERS
The Last Black and White Midnight Movie

Clive James Looks at the Cinema Screen

The movie that most moved me this month may take more money than multi-millionaire mystery-man hideaway Howard Hughes himself. It's a human interest picture; the sort that makes you concentrate on the usherette. Ouch. Joking apart, all motion picture addicts worthy of the name should pin back their eyeballs and take a celluloid shower in this one. If you can't tell the difference between Zsa Zsa Gabor, and you don't much care, it may not be exactly your cup of possum juice, but catch it if you can for the sheer magic of the Intermission which comes like a dose of clap in the middle of a mad month in a Melbourne cat-house. The name of the picture escapes me.

'Rayner's Lane' is a movie you'd be well advised to miss. And you'd be wrong. Go and see it. You'll be surprised. It's terrible. It's definitely mutton dressed as Lady Caroline Lamb but I haven't had such an enjoyable time in the cinema since I spent four hours in a Sydney Drive-In and finally discovered it was a multi-storey car park. Ouch.

The same goes for 'The Con'. Don't miss it. Avoid it like the plague. But go anyway. You'll hate it. It's marvellous. It's Kafka in a sheep dip, an example of the Protestant Work Ethic on Rollerskates with

197

enough acres of fresh flesh to bring a boyish smile to the frozen features
of a case-hardened Bushman at an outback cattle auction. But enough
– as Kierkegaard observed – is a treat. Don't take your family, take
your mac. Personally I'd rather drink warm Fosters, but, as W. H.
Auden said, 'It takes two to tango.' He should know. Ouch.

'Lovesick' makes 'Claire's Knee' look like a rare skin disease. Catch
it at your peril. It's a skin-flic for dermatologists only. If you're an
osteopath with a warped sense of humour and your own sauna bath,
you might just like it. If not, be warned. Go and see it. You'll hate it.
It's smashing. No sweat, but all armpit. Ouch. Like sodomy, it's fun
once in a while but let's hope they don't make it compulsory. It's
rather like being offered a choice between drowning to death in a cup
of cold vomit, while eating skewered eyeballs, or being beaten about
the brain with a de luxe edition of *Roget's Thesaurus* while nibbling at
nourishing roast fingernails. Not a choice I'd care to make. But if
pushed – plump for the fingernails. Goodnight. Ouch.

MONTY PYTHON
The Brand New Monty Python Papperbok

War

. . . GODFREY *looks around and sees a group of Japanese Soldiers wearing
Sony headphones.*

HARRY KIRI *has a row of pocket calculators in place of medals.*

GODFREY. Where am I?

KIRI. You are in the canton of Mitzebushi, formerly Milton Keynes.
We here to protect consumer of Japanese product. You come with
me yes please.

A Japanese factory compound with wire fence. GODFREY *is lined up with
several others, facing* HARRY KIRI *, who is standing on a platform in front of a
pre-fab wearing a Sony Walkman.*

KIRI. My name is Kiri. Harry Kiri. Haw, haw. Old Samurai joke.

No reaction.

Ah. Where is famous British humour now? Answer – in Tokyo. John Cleese very big in Japan. Now you all work very hard like dogs. If you very good, you work for five years and get pocket calculator. (*Tapping his row of calculators.*)

AN AUSTRALIAN. What about some food, you yellow bastard?

KIRI. Food make you fat. Very bad for spirit of work. Japanese work twenty-six hours a day and live in cupboard with mother-in-law. She so thin, when she cross the road to feed chicken, her arse fall in river. Haw, haw, haw. Oh yes. Very old Japanese joke . . . Any question?

One of the prisoners collapses. A north country man, HOVIS, *steps forward.*

HOVIS. Excuse me, your Imperial Highness.

KIRI (*removing headphones*). Pardon?

HOVIS. With reference to er, rule twelve, paragraph three, as er, shop steward, I officially withdraw my labour.

KIRI. Very well, Mr Hovis. You spend two weeks' annual holiday now in car boot.

He clicks his fingers. Two guards also wearing Sony Walkmans take HOVIS *to the corner of the compound. There is a mound with a car boot sticking out of it, surrounded by a barbed wire fence. They open the boot.*

AUSTRALIAN. Good luck, Pommy.

HOVIS. Vote Labour.

Cheers from the prisoners. The guards shut him in the boot.

KIRI. Anyone else for annual holidays now?

The prisoners and GODFREY *are working on the production line, whistling the theme from 'Bridge On the River Kwai'. Guards walk up and down. Two British officers are talking furtively.*

FIELD MARSHAL. Jenkins.

JENKINS. Yes, sir.

199

FIELD MARSHAL. We've got to do something to help the war effort. We've got to slow things up.

JENKINS. Yes, sir.

They look around warily and give signals to the others. They all start whistling at half speed.

All the prisoners are filing into their hut. HARRY KIRI *stands in the doorway, with a tray of tea. He blows a whistle.*

KIRI. Time for tea-so-strong-filthy-spoon-stand-up-in-it ceremony.

He goes out. The Australian goes to a crack in the door and peers out. He gives the thumbs up.

AUSTRALIAN. OK. Let's go.

They all spring into action. Two men unscrew the front of a 'Space Invaders' machine and disappear through it.

You coming with us, Godfrey?

GODFREY. Are you digging a tunnel?

AUSTRALIAN. Too right, digger. We've just built ourselves a whole bloody subway system.

He turns round a map of the London Underground and points at it.

We're linking up here with the Northern Line.

GODFREY. That's amazing!

AUSTRALIAN. You'd better meet Jenkins and get togged out.

They go to the other end of the hut.

This is Godfrey, sir. He wants to come with us.

JENKINS. Hello.

AUSTRALIAN. When you've finished here, go and see the Captain over there.

He goes. JENKINS *picks up a list.*

JENKINS. Right. What do you want to be, Godfrey? Guard or commuter?

GODFREY. Er . . . I'll go as a commuter.

JENKINS *(studying* GODFREY*).* Ummm. You look the young executive type to me. Probably lives in Morden, er. . . drives a Volvo estate and beats his wife at weekends. You know the sort.

He hands GODFREY *a bowler hat and a brolly.*

Had a bit of a job with this one. Made it out of old Marmite pots, ha.

GODFREY. It looks very real.

The AUSTRALIAN, *with headband and guitar, comes over.*

AUSTRALIAN. How does this look, sir?

JENKINS. Well, you should pass as a busker. Yes, should be all right. Show me one of your busking tunes, corporal.

AUSTRALIAN *(sings).*
Let me take you by the hand,
And lead you through the streets of London . . .

JENKINS. Yes, yes. That should do the trick splendidly. Remember to keep your eyes on the ground and sing through your nose. That way you should be all right. Next.

A Field Marshal wearing tartan cheese cutter and scarf steps forward.

Ah, Field Marshal. How are you doing with your Scottish football fan?

FIELD MARSHAL *(pretending to be drunk).* Eh! Two-nil, you bastard.

He nuts JENKINS .

201

JENKINS. Well done, sir. That should do the trick.

GODFREY *is talking to the* CAPTAIN .

CAPTAIN. Right, let's go through this again. A guard approaches you in the train and demands to see your ticket. What is your reaction?

GODFREY. I say, er, 'Go back to where you came from, you black bastard.'

CAPTAIN. Very good. Now. Here's one ticket to Pinner, one brown paper bag with bondage photos and one copy of . . .

A man by the window makes a 'Space Invaders' start signal.

MAN. Deedle doo da.

The signal is repeated all down the hut to the 'Space Invaders' machine. Two men standing beside it spring into action and pretend to play the machine, making all the rocket and explosion noises. The others rush around concealing things. HARRY KIRI *enters. The prisoners all act over-natural. Two are playing a fast game of chess.*

FIELD MARSHAL. Checkmate. Your move.

JENKINS *and the* CAPTAIN *are singing and dancing a funky disco number. One is pretending to be the director.*

JENKINS *and* CAPTAIN.
  Get down on that funky beat,
  Get on down that funky street . . .

CAPTAIN. No, no, sir. It's 'Get down *on* that funky beat'. Let's do it again.

HARRY KIRI *looks around him. Satisfied, he walks towards the door. He stops and sees a yellow tube ticket on the floor. The hut goes silent. He picks it up and turns to* GODFREY .

KIRI. What is this yellow thing?

GODFREY. Er ... custard.

KIRI (*looking at the ticket*). Ah. Oxford Circus custard. Famous English delicacy. (*He puts it in his mouth.*) Umm. Tastes like Mother's Pride.

He goes out. JENKINS *slaps* GODFREY *on the back.*

JENKINS. Phew. Well done, Godfrey. That was pretty close.

AUSTRALIAN. Yeah . . . never thought he'd swallow that one! (*He laughs loudly.*)

JENKINS. Look, we'd better move fast. There's very little time to lose . . . .

PETER RICHARDSON AND PETER RICHENS
The Comic Strip Presents . . . .

PROSAIC

PROSAIC

The Sublime and the Ridiculous

Among our leading novelists, some are prolific, some less so. There must be many readers of Miss Iris Murdoch who live in fear of a fallow year, when no more than one novel by the author drops from her pen, leaving them with long empty evenings to waste. The following extract, from a new work called The Sublime and the Ridiculous, *is designed to cater for this eventuality, by having many characters, some of them hardly used at all, who can – under fresh titles like* The Necessary *and* The Contingent *or* The Many *and* The Few *– be put through fresh permutations by bereft readers on rainy days.*

'Flavia says that Hugo tells her that Augustina is in love with Fred.'

Sir Alex Mountaubon stood with his wife Lavinia in one of the deeply recessed mullion windows of the long gallery at Bishop's Breeches, looking out at the topiary peacocks on the terrace beyond. In front of them the fountain, topped with statuary in which a naked Mars played joyously with a willing Venus, gently coruscated, its tinkle audible through the open windows. The scene before them was of order and peace. They could look down the park at the mile-long drive of lindens, the colour of jaundice; to one side, away from its necessary order, stood one dark and contingent cedar tree. Beneath it their older daughter, Flavia, could be seen from the window, sitting on a white wooden seat, in her unutterable otherness, her pet marmoset on her shoulder, her cap of auburn hair shining like burnished gold on her head. Nearer to the house, in the rose-garden, their younger daughter, seven-year-old Perdita, strange, mysterious and self-absorbed as usual, was beheading a litter of puppies with unexpectedly muscular and adult twists of her slender arm. Her cap of golden hair shone like burnished auburn on her head.

Alex turned, catching sight of himself in the big, gilt, rather battered cupid-encrusted mirror that soared over the mantel. Mortality was there in the darkened eyes, but most of what he saw there, the solid, round face of a man of principle, pleased him exceedingly. His book, a philosophical study of Niceness, was almost complete; in its writing Lavinia, his second wife, had proved the perfect helpmeet and companion. No one lay dying upstairs. He looked around at the familiar objects, the Titians and Tintorettos, glowing in their serried ranks with jewelled beneficence, the twined, golden forms of bodies twisted together suggesting a radiant vision of another world. In cases stood the Sung cups, the Ting plates, the Tang vases, the Ming statuettes, the Ching saucers; these last must, almost certainly, go.

'Who says whom tells her that who is in love with whom?'

Lavinia, her arms full of lilies, did not turn. 'Flavia,' she said.

'And are they?'

'They think so. I don't think they quite know.'

'But at least we know. About us,' said Alex lovingly. He looked out of the window and saw Perdita staring strangely up at the house; and suddenly, involuntarily, he recalled again that experience of utter freedom he had known for the first time when he and Moira LeBenedictus had lain naked together in the Reading Room of the British Museum, after hours of course; he, as a senior civil servant, had been entitled to a key. Other moments came back: Moira walking through Harrods without her shoes, Moira on the night they had boxed together on the roof of St Paul's Cathedral, Moira threatening him in the Tottenham Hotspurs football ground at midnight with her whaler's harpoon.

Two miles away, in the bathroom at his house, Buttocks, Sir Hugo Occam laid down his razor. He walked through into the bedroom where Moira LeBenedictus lay. She was his good towards which he magnetically swung. She lay on the bed, gathering her hair together into a cap of black.

'Are we acting rightly?'

'I think we are,' she said.

'Oh, Moira.'

'Come, come, Hugo,' she said. From the alcove, Leo Chatteris, a spoiled priest, long in love with Moira, watched them in protective benediction. Could he surrender her? The pain was so much he knew it was right . . . .

MALCOLM BRADBURY

From Too Late *or* Edward Ferguson
by Russell Morm [or Somerset Maugham]

Stumbling, groping he took the homeward path between the coco-nut and the pandanus trees. Just where the way forked to run steeply upwards towards the white bungalow, he stumbled over something soft, and fell again. The body of Uiala lay across the road. She had thrust the long blade of her *sarong* into her heart.

He rose and staggered on blindly, not upwards, but down, down towards the lagoon. There was only one thing left to do. He would swim out into the shark-infested waters, infested with sharks, and there find peace.

E.V. KNOX
Fiction as She is Wrote

On Dr Johnson Not Being Depicted on the Back of a £1 Note

BOSWELL. I must say I consider it remiss of government not to honour one of the greatest of Englishmen in this fashion.

JOHNSON. *Honour!* – you must be jesting, sir. This present practice of emblazening the eminent upon the backs of their trumpery bank-notes is one of the most breath-takingly brazen expedients devised even by this craven crew of egregious mountebanks . . . .

JON FERNSIDE

Scruts
[after Arnold Bennett]

Emily Wrackgarth stirred the Christmas pudding till her right arm began to ache. But she did not cease for that. She stirred on till her right arm grew so numb that it might have been the right arm of some girl at the other end of Bursley. And yet something deep down in her whispered, 'It is *your* right arm! And you can do what you like with it!'

She did what she liked with it. Relentlessly she kept it moving till it reasserted itself as the arm of Emily Wrackgarth, prickling and tingling as with red-hot needles in every tendon from wrist to elbow. And still Emily Wrackgarth hardened her heart.

Presently she saw the spoon no longer revolving, but wavering aimlessly in the midst of the basin. Ridiculous! This must be seen to! In the down of dark hairs that connected her eyebrows there was a marked deepening of that vertical cleft which, visible at all times, warned you that here was a young woman not to be trifled with. Her brain despatched to her hand a peremptory message – which miscarried. The spoon wabbled as though held by a baby. Emily knew that she herself as a baby had been carried into this very kitchen to stir the Christmas pudding. Year after year, as she grew up, she had been allowed to stir it 'for luck'. And those, she reflected, were the only cookery lessons she ever got. How like Mother! . . .

At mid-day, when her brother came home from the Works, she was still at it.

'Brought those scruts with you?' she asked, without looking up.

'That's a fact,' he said, dipping his hand into the sagging pocket of his coat.

It is perhaps necessary to explain what scruts are. In the daily output of every potbank there are a certain proportion of flawed vessels. These are cast aside by the foreman, with a lordly gesture, and in due course are hammered into fragments. These fragments, which are put to various uses, are called scruts; and one of the uses they are put to is a sentimental one. The dainty and luxurious Southerner looks to find in his Christmas pudding a wedding-ring, a gold thimble, a threepenny-bit, or the like. To such fal-lals the Five Towns would say fie. A Christmas pudding in the Five Towns contains nothing but suet, flour, lemon-peel, cinnamon, brandy, almonds, raisins – and two or three scruts. There is a world of poetry, beauty, romance, in scruts – though you have to have been brought up on them to appreciate it. Scruts have passed into the proverbial philosophy of the district. 'Him's a pudden with more scruts than raisins to 'm' is a criticism not infrequently heard. It implies respect, even admiration. Of Emily Wrackgarth herself people often said, in reference to her likeness to her father, 'Her's a scrut o' th'owd basin.' . . .

'By the by,' said Jos, 'you remember Albert Grapp? I have asked him to step over from Hanbridge and help eat our snack on Christmas Day.'

Emily gave Jos one of her looks. 'You've asked that Mr Grapp?'

'No objection, I hope? He's not a bad sort. And he's considered a bit of a ladies' man, you know.'

She gathered up all the scruts and let them fall in a rattling shower on the exiguous pudding. Two or three fell wide of the basin. These she added.

'Steady on!' cried Jos. 'What's that for?'

'That's for your guest,' replied his sister. 'And if you think you're going to palm me off onto him, or on to any other young fellow, you're a fool, Jos Wrackgarth.' . . .

MAX BEERBOHM

Tough at the Top
by John Braine

I dipped into the pocket of my suit – it was an eighteen-ounce quince-coloured safari-style barathea, and cost me seventy-nine pounds from the best boutique in Leddersford – and offered her a John Player Special. Then, when my Braun butane flickered, I turned away from the wheel, and looked straight into her Mary Quant face. 'Aye, things have changed,' I said, in the flat northern accent I use when I'm with very expensive people, 'You've got to have progress, haven't you?' Laetitia, Marchioness of Salop, *was* expensive; you'd only to glance at her to see that. Her body was like that of a pet cocker spaniel fed on Lotameat, fine, trim, shining, well-brushed; and you could tell at a glance that everything around her was dedicated to keeping it that way. She put her hand lightly on my wrist, touching my Omega digital; I could smell the fresh scent of her Badedas. 'Say progress again, Joe,' she said, 'I just love your round Rs.' 'I like yours too, love,' I said . . . .

MALCOLM BRADBURY

Lawrence Examines the British Museum Reading Room

He passed through the narrow vaginal passage, and entered the huge womb of the Reading Room. Across the floor, dispersed along the radiating desks, scholars curled, foetus-like, over their books, little buds

211

of intellectual life thrown off by some gigantic act of generation performed upon that nest of knowledge, those inexhaustible ovaries of learning, the concentric inner rings of the catalogue shelves.

The circular wall of the Reading Room wrapped the scholars in a protective layer of books, while above them arched the vast, distended belly of the dome. Little daylight entered through the grimy glass at the top. No sounds of traffic or other human business penetrated to that warm, airless space. The dome looked down on the scholars, and the scholars looked down on their books; and the scholars loved their books, stroking the pages with soft pale fingers. The pages responded to the fingers' touch, and yielded their knowledge gladly to the scholars, who collected it in little boxes of file-cards. When the scholars raised their eyes from their desks they saw nothing to distract them, nothing out of harmony with their books, only the smooth, curved lining of the womb. Wherever the eye travelled, it met no arrest, no angle, no parallel lines receding into infinity, no pointed arch striving towards the unattainable: all was curved, rounded, self-sufficient, complete. And the scholars dropped their eyes to their books again, fortified and consoled. They curled themselves more tightly over their books, for they did not want to leave the warm womb, where they fed upon electric light and inhaled the musty odour of yellowing pages . . . .

DAVID LODGE
The British Museum is Falling Down

A's Trials

[A, presumably an acquaintance of Kafka's K, attempts to renew his British Museum Reading Room ticket.]

Adam, or A as he would now more vaguely have identified himself, had been all through this before, but could not be sure whether he had dreamed it or actually experienced it. He was trapped. Behind him was a locked, guarded door; in front of him a long corridor terminating in a room. He could not go back. He could not stay where he was – the men in the room at the end of the corridor, warned by the bell, were expecting him. He went reluctantly forward, down the long corridor, between the smooth polished wooden cabinets, locked and inscrutable, which formed the walls, stretching high out of reach. Craning his neck to see if they reached the high ceiling, A felt suddenly dizzy, and leaned against the wall for support.

The room at the end of the corridor was an office, with a long, curving counter behind which sat two men, neat, self-possessed, expectant. A approached the nearer man, who immediately began writing on a piece of paper.

'Yes? he said, after a few minutes had passed, and without looking up.

A, his mouth unaccountably dry, enunciated with difficulty the words, 'Reading Room Ticket.'

'Over there.'

A sidled along the counter to the second man, who immediately began writing in a ledger. A waited patiently.

'Yes?' said the second man, closing his ledger with a snap that made A jump.

'IwanttorenewmyReadingRoomTicket,' gabbled A.

'Over there.'

'But I've just been over there. He sent me to you.' Out of the corner of his eye, A saw the first man watching them intently.

The second man scrutinised him for what seemed a very long time, then spoke. 'One moment.' He went over to the first man, and they held a whispered conference, at the conclusion of which the first man came over to A and sat down in the second man's seat.

'What is it you want, exactly?' he asked.

'I want to renew my Reading Room Ticket,' said A patiently.

'You want to *renew* it? You mean you have a ticket already?'

'Yes'.

'May I see it?'

A presented his ticket.

'It's out of date,' observed the man.

'That's why I want to renew it!' A exclaimed.

'When did you last use the Reading Room?'

'Two months ago,' lied A, cunningly.

'You haven't used it since your ticket expired?'

'No.'

'It wouldn't matter if you had,' said the man. 'As long as you're not lying.' He tore A's ticket neatly into four sections, and deposited them in a waste-paper basket. It distressed A to see his ticket torn up. He experienced a queasy, empty feeling in his stomach.

213

'So now you want to renew your annual ticket?'

'Please.'

'You see, you didn't make that clear to me just now.'

'I'm sorry.'

'I assumed you were a casual reader wanting a short-term ticket. That's why I sent you to my colleague.' He nodded in the direction of the second man. 'But when he realised you wanted an annual ticket, he directed you back to me. That is the reason for our apparently contradictory behaviour.'

He flashed a sudden smile, displaying a row of gold-filled teeth.

'I see. I'm afraid it was my fault,' A apologised.

'Don't mention it,' said the first man, opening the ledger and beginning to write.

'Could I have my new ticket now?' said A, after some minutes had passed.

'Over there.'

'But you just said you were responsible for renewing annual tickets!' protested A.

'Ah, but that was when I was sitting over there,' said the first man. 'We've changed places now. We do that from time to time. So that if one of us should fall ill,' he continued, 'the other can cover his work.'

A made his way wearily to the second man.

'Good morning. Can I help you?' said the second man, as if greeting him for the first time.

'I want to renew my annual Reading Room ticket,' said A.

'Certainly. May I see your old ticket?'

'No, the other man – gentleman – has just torn it up.'

'It *was* an annual ticket you had?'

'Yes. He just tore it up. Didn't you see him?'

The second man shook his head gravely. 'This is very irregular. You shouldn't have given him the ticket. He's on short-term tickets now.'

'Look, all I want is to have my ticket renewed. What does it matter which of you does it?'

'I'm afraid I can't renew a ticket which, as far as I'm concerned, doesn't exist.'

A gripped the counter tightly and closed his eyes. 'What do you suggest I do then?' he whispered hoarsely.

'I could give you a short-term ticket . . . .'

'No that won't do. I'm working here every day. My livelihood depends upon my being here every day.'

'Then I can only suggest that you come back when my colleague and I have changed places again,' said the second man.

'When will that be?'

'Oh there's no telling. You can wait if you like . . . .'

DAVID LODGE
The British Museum is Falling Down

Cold Comfort Farm
[after Mary Webb and others]

In the large kitchen, which occupied most of the middle of the house, a sullen fire burned, the smoke of which wavered up the blackened walls and over the deal table, darkened by age and dirt, which was roughly set for a meal. A snood full of coarse porridge hung over the fire, and standing with one arm resting upon the high mantel, looking moodily down into the heaving contents of the snood, was a tall young man whose riding-boots were splashed with mud to the thigh, and whose coarse linen shirt was open to his waist. The firelight lit up his diaphragm muscles as they heaved slowly in rough rhythm with the porridge.

He looked up as Judith entered, and gave a short, defiant laugh, but said nothing. Judith crossed slowly over until she stood by his side. She was as tall as he. They stood in silence, she staring at him, and he down into the secret crevasses of the porridge.

'Well, mother mine,' he said at last, 'here I am, you see. I said I would be in time for breakfast, and I have kept my word.'

His voice had a low, throaty, animal quality, a sneering warmth that wound a velvet ribbon of sexuality over the outward coarseness of the man.

Judith's breath came in long shudders. She thrust her arms deeper into her shawl. The porridge gave an ominous leering heave; it might almost have been endowed with life, so uncannily did its movements keep pace with the human passions that throbbed above it.

'Cur,' said Judith, levelly, at last. 'Coward! Liar! Libertine! Who were you with last night? Moll at the mill or Violet at the vicarage? Or Ivy, perhaps, at the ironmongery? Seth – my son . . . .' Her deep, dry voice quivered, but she whipped it back, and her next words flew out at him like a lash.

215

'Do you want to break my heart?'

'Yes,' said Seth, with an elemental simplicity.

The porridge boiled over . . . .

STELLA GIBBONS

Mrs Dalloway's Clock
[after Virginia Woolf]

An expectant hush had fallen on the scene. From nearby Westminster, Mrs Dalloway's clock boomed out the half hour. It partook, Adam thought, shifting his weight in the saddle, of metempsychosis, the way his humble life fell into moulds prepared by literature. Or was it, he wondered, picking his nose, the result of closely studying the sentence structure of the English novelists? One had resigned oneself to having no private language any more, but one had clung wistfully to the illusion of a personal property of events. A fond and fruitless illusion, it seemed, for here, inevitably, came the limousine, with its Very Important Personage, or Personages, dimly visible in the interior. The policeman saluted, and the crowd pressed forward, murmuring, 'Philip', 'Tony and Margaret', 'Prince Andrew'.

DAVID LODGE
The British Museum is Falling Down

The Peculiar Bird
[after H.G. Wells]

''Eng!'' said Mr Bottleby, addressing the eighteenth milestone with intense bitterness: ''Eng!''

The bright windy sunshine on that open downland road, the sense of healthy effort, of rhythmic trundling speed, the consciousness of the nearly new ready-to-wear gent's cycling costume which draped his limbs – it had been ticketed 'ENORMOUS REDUCTION ', and, underneath that again, 'STARTLING SACRIFICE , 25/6', in Parkinson's great front window on the South Parade – none of these things had availed

216

to dissipate the gradual gloom which had been settling like a miasma on Mr Bottleby's mind through the whole of that morning of May. Various causes, historical, social as well as physiological, had contributed their share towards that tenebrous exhalation which already seemed to hang about him like a tangible and visible cloud. But undoubtedly its immediate origin and the cause of his hasty flight was the state of the Breakfast Bacon. Greasy. Uneatable. Tck! How many times had he told Ann, a hundred times if he had told her once, that he liked it in little crisp hard pieces and the eggs poached separately on toast? He was Fed Up. That was it. Absobloominglutely Fed. Tck!

If some well-meaning social philosopher had attempted to explain to Mr Bottleby the exact processes whereby a wasteful and ill-organised civilisation had condemned him to struggle Laocoon-like in the coils of the retail ironmongery and the embraces of an uncongenial spouse, it is doubtful whether Mr Bottleby would have clearly understood. But his resentment against fate was none the less profound because it was largely inarticulate and because he would probably have summed up all this mismanagement and stupidity and carelessness and insensate cruelty in some simple epigram like 'A bit too thick.' Vaguely, in the recesses of his being, Mr Bottleby knew that in some way or other there ought to have been for him a more beautiful and gracious existence, a life somehow different from the drudgery and pettiness that he endured . . . .

''Eng!' repeated Mr Bottleby to the nineteenth milestone; ''Eng!'

And having come now to the rather precipitous winding lane which leads down into Fittlehurst village he placed his feet on the rests — it was long before the luxurious days of the free-wheel — folded his arms and began to coast. Perilously, but with a certain sense of satisfaction in his extreme recklessness, to coast . . . .

One figures him, a slightly rotund shape of about three-and-thirty years of age, attired in the check knickerbocker suit which had meant such an earthshaking sacrifice to Mr Parkinson; one figures him, I say, with his freckled face, pleasant brown eyes and that large tuft of hair which continually escaped the control of his cap peak, rushing rapidly, worried, tormented by destiny, between those tall hedges on which the hawthorn had already made patches of scented, almost delirious, bloom, rushing downwards — on . . . .

Whuck!

I come now upon a difficulty. I find it exceedingly hard to describe to you the nature of that surprising existence to which Mr Bottleby awoke when, having caught the fallen telegraph wire – fallen in yesterday's gale so that it blocked the Fittlehurst road like a piece of paddock fencing – having caught this wire exactly under his chin, he was projected out and away into the Ultimate Beyond . . . .

E.V. KNOX

George Orwell and the Postal System

A feature of English life is the large bookshop. There must be about thirty of these in London alone, and I have no doubt that there are others in the provinces. In appearance they are pretty much the same: a few shelves stacked with the latest novels, a table of war memoirs and biography, a department devoted to children's books and probably a basement festooned with the latest paperbacks (Penguin, Panther, Four Square etc etc).

In recent months most, if not all, of these shops have begun to stock certain red-coloured volumes perhaps two inches thick and weighing about half a pound each. (This is guesswork – I have no kitchen scales.) These books are usually displayed in sets of four. They are all volumes of the same work – the Collected Essays, Journalism and Letters of George Orwell. They cost £2.50p each, so that a set of four would cost roughly £10. The appeal of these books is clear. They are aimed at readers who, for one reason or another, want to own the Collected Essays, Journalism and Letters of George Orwell.

Who Orwell is I have no idea. The name is evidently a pseudonym, and probably he does not exist. It seems unlikely that a collection totalling 2,041 pages could be the work of the same person. Presumably Orwell is a trade name reserved by the publishers for this kind of thing.

Next to bubble-gum cards, these books of Orwell's give us probably the most reliable index to what is really important in England today. It is well worth getting hold of them and examining the contents. Discounting introductions, appendices and so on, the four books consist of five hundred and three items of differing lengths ranging from half a page to fifty-three pages. Putting aside various essays and other bits and pieces, they can be broken down in the following way:

218

Poems   4
Prefaces   4
Diaries   5
Book reviews   64
Letters   251

What is immediately plain is that there are four times as many letters as book reviews, and sixty-two times more letters than poems. Even if one includes the essays and bits and pieces, the letters still account for fractionally under fifty per cent of the total number of items. It is evidently as a letter-writer that Orwell has made his mark on the middle-class public – the journalists, lawyers, politicians, gentlemen farmers and the like who take in his stuff. His publishers would not think it worthwhile to charge £10 for the four volumes if this were not so. They know their market.

Orwell's style as a correspondent is no better and no worse than a score of others in the same *genre*. The following are fair samples:

Dear Cyril,
    I see from the N.S. & N. list that you have a book coming out sometime this spring. If you can manage to get a copy sent to me I'll review it.

Here is one to someone else:

Dear Spender,
    I hope things go well with you.

The first thing that anyone would notice about these letters is that they are private. The ones I have quoted are entirely typical. The familiarity 'Dear Cyril' is repeated over and over again, and so is 'Dear Dennis' (three times), 'Dear Tony' (ten) and 'My dear Runciman.' What the letters do is to satisfy the English weakness for reading other people's mail. It is ridiculous to suppose that this is not an English characteristic, especially of the upper middle class. It probably dates from the Penny Post Act of 1840. For the first time the common people, the servants, livery-men, stable-boys and others, were able to communicate with each other without fear of being overheard by Lord This or Lord That. The propertied classes have always misunderstood the danger to them of social change, and so they imagined that the threat would come from an organised Left. Fearing revolution, they began to read their servants' mail. Even a cursory glance at Victorian literature will show how the habit infiltrated down to the middle and lower middle classes. I can think off-hand of a score of cheap railway novels where the plot revolves on a letter falling into the wrong hands.

This explains the popularity of Orwell's letters, but it is important to ask another question, and that is why they were made public in the first place. After all, publishing is only a trade like any other, and Secker and Warburg (Orwell's publishers) could have made just as much money by putting out cheap reprints or pornography. There is one point about the Orwell letters that is significant – the date. They were published about the same time, probably even in the same month, as the two-tier postal system was introduced. It was vitally necessary for the Government to get the English masses 'letter-minded,' otherwise the two-tier scheme could not have worked. The release of the Orwell letters at this time was only a minor move, but it succeeded in getting the English people to think favourably about letters, and thus about the postal system. That presumably was the calculation.

Now it is absurd to deduce from this that there was any collusion between Orwell, Secker and Warburg and the Postmaster-General. To call Orwell a government lackey is to suggest a sinister plot that simply does not exist. Secker and Warburg are, so far as I know, reputable men, and the Postmaster-General is at worst an ineffectual ass. There was no sinister plot. That is not how the English political system works. In this country it is enough for the ruling classes to make their wishes known, and men like Secker, Warburg and Orwell will *instinctively* do what is required of them. For what conceivable reason shouldn't they? I have no idea how much they make a year out of this letters business, but it must be a sizeable sum. It would be childish to expect them not to support the Post Office for all they are worth. There is a strong case for thinking that the system under which Orwell and Co flourished should be altered. What there is no case for is to denounce Orwell and his like for behaving as they do. That is simply an example of British hypocrisy, and the sort of thing for which Europeans, who at any rate understand the function of the English postman, justifiably despise us.

KEITH WATERHOUSE

For Whom the Gong Sounds
With apologies, somewhat, to Mr Hemingway

The mouth of the cave was camouflaged by a curtain of saddle-blankets, matadores' capes and the soles of old espadrilles. Inside it smelt of man-sweat, acrid and brown ... horse-sweat sweet and magenta. There was the leathery smell of leather and the coppery smell of copper and borne in on the clear night air came the distant smell of skunk.

The wife of Pablo was stirring frijoles in a Catalonian wineskin. She wore rope-soled shoes and a belt of hand grenades. Over her magnificent buttocks swung a sixteenth-century cannon taken from the Escorial.

'I obscenity in the obscenity of thy unprintable obscenity,' said Pilar.

'This is the Ingles of the street car. He of the boardwalk to come soon.'

'I obscenity in the unprintable of the milk of all street cars.' The woman was stirring the steaming mess with the horns of a Mura bull. She stared at Robert Jordan then smiled. 'Obscenity, obscenity, obscenity,' she said, not unkindly.

'Qué va,' said Robert Jordan. 'Bueno. Good.'

'Menos mal,' said El Sordo. 'Not so good.'

'Go unprint thyself,' said Pilar. The gypsy went outside and unprinted himself.

The girl with the shaved head filled a tin pail full of petite marmite and handed it to him and she gave him a great swig from the wine-skin and he chewed the succulent bits of horsemeat and they said nothing.

And now Esteban stood beside him on the rim of the gorge. This is it, Robert Jordan said to himself. I believe this is it. I did not think it was this to be it but it seems to be it, all right. Robert Jordan spat down the gorge. Pablo watched the fast disappearing globule of man-saliva then slowly, softly spat down the gorge. Pilar said obscenity thy saliva then she too spat down the gorge. This time it was Pablo's gorge.

The girl was walking beside him.

'Hola, Ingles,' she said. 'Hello, English.'

'Equally, guapa,' said Robert Jordan.

'Qué va,' said the girl.

'Rabbit.'

Robert Jordan pulled the pistol lanyard up, cocked his maquina and tightened the ropes of his rope-soled shoes.

'Vamos,' he said, 'Let's go.'

'Si,' said Maria. 'Yes.'

They walked on in silence until they came to a rocky ledge. There were rough rocks and thistles and a wild growth of Spanish dagger. Robert Jordan spread his buffalo robe out for himself and allowed Maria to lie near him on a bed of nettles. The earth moved.

'Rabbit,' said Robert Jordan. 'Hast aught?'

'Nay, naught.'

'Maria,' he said. 'Mary. Little shaved head.'

'Let me go with thee and be thy rabbit.'

The earth moved again. This time it was a regular earthquake. Californians would have called it a temblor.

Robert Jordan had reached the boardwalk. He lay in the gorse and rubble. He had his infernal machine beside him, some hand grenades, a blunderbuss, an arquebus and a greyhound bus. His maquina was held securely in his teeth. Across the ravine Anselmo was sniping off sentries as they passed.

Listen, Robert Jordan said to himself, only the fascist bombs made so much noise he couldn't hear. You had to do what you did. If you don't do what you do now you'll never do what you do now. Now now you won't. Sure it does. He lashed the wire through the rings of the cotter pins of the release levers of the wires of the main spring of the coil, insulating it with a piece cut off the bottom of his rope-soled shoes.

What about the others . . . Eladio and Ignacio . . . Anselmo and St Elmo? And Rabbit? I wonder how Rabbit is. Stop that now. This is no time to think about Rabbit . . . . Or rabbits. Better think about something else. Think about llamas. It's better to breathe, he thought. It's always much better to breathe. Sure it is. The time was gradually, inevitably drawing near. Someone in the valley was singing an old Catalonian song. A plane crashed quietly overhead. Robert Jordan lay still and listened for the gong to sound . . . .

CORNELIA OTIS SKINNER

PARTLY

$\boxed{\times}$

POLITICAL

Party Political Speech

SPEAKER. My friends, in the light of present-day developments, let me say right away that I do not regard existing conditions likely. On the contrary, I have always regarded them as subjects of the gravest responsibility, and shall ever continue to do so. Indeed, I will even go further and state quite categorically that I am more than sensible of the definition of the precise issues which are at this moment concerning us all. We must build, but we must build surely. *('Hear, hear'; applause.)* Let me say just this. If any part of what I say is challenged, then I am more than ready to meet that challenge, for I have no doubt whatsoever that whatever I have said in the past, or what I am saying now is the exact, literal and absolute truth as to the state of the case. *(Applause.)* I put it to you that this is not a time for vague promises of better things to come, for if I were to convey to you a spirit of false optimism then I should be neither fair to you nor true to myself. But does this mean, I hear you cry, that we can no longer look forward to the future that it is to come? Certainly not!

MAX SCHREINER

Speaking as a Friend of His . . . .

The following statement was almost certainly issued last night by a person who wishes to remain anonymous:

'In the light of certain statements which have been made, and of the circumstances surrounding those statements, I feel that the time has come to clear the air. Although it has become progressively more difficult for me to remain silent I much regret that the necessity for intervention should have arisen in present conditions. However, in view of the currency given, wisely or unwisely, to matters which can only be conjectural I have thought it best to set the record straight.

'In deciding to issue this statement I have therefore had regard both to the nature of the speculation which has taken place and in particular to the clear duty which is incumbent upon all of us to make our positions plain so that there can be no misunderstanding in future as there has been, regrettably in my view, in the past. This duty is especially clear when, as in the present case, allegations have been ventilated without a sufficient knowledge of the context in which they should be considered.

'In the prevailing situation, and as a result of information which has been published, albeit in an incomplete form, it would be wrong to prejudge the issue. That is emphatically not my intention, but I hope that this clarification of the questions involved will help to place them in a proper perspective. It is in the interest of everybody concerned that unverified suppositions should be answered in the clearest detail, and I trust that this statement will have achieved that effect.'

A spokesman said later that he had no comment to make on the statement.

THE GUARDIAN

The Chancellor of the Exchequer

Good evening. I am here tonight to talk to you on a purely non-political, non-partisan, Labour party basis. I am the Chancellor of the Exchequer . . . .

Now, a lot of people have been saying recently that our economy is in really bad shape. Really? Yes. Bad? Yes. Shape? Perhaps. But really bad shape? (Pause.) Now then. Let's get down to brass tacks. The brass tax which I shall be imposing is an expedient necessity. It is essential, at this time, when our beloved country has its back to the wall, to realise how heartening that can be. Only with one's back to the wall can one go forward . . . to the next wall. People often come up to me in the street, which is in itself encouraging. They say, 'Look here, Smartypants' – and let us not forget that 'Look here, Smartypants' is what democracy is all about – 'Look here, what about the pound?' A fair question. A good question . . . and one that I intend to dispense with altogether tonight. I put the issues squarely before you. One, the pound is stable. The horse may have gone, but the pound is stable.

Two, I wouldn't be doing this job if I were not a trained economist and mathematician. Five, my policy is one of non-alignment. I will not see Britain's money spent – on your behalf. Six, the Prime Minister is behind me – always. *(He looks round nervously.)* Seven, the trade index for the last fiscal year shows a trend that can only be described. And eight, figures prove nothing. That is why I say to you, this is a time for you, and I, and him, to tighten our belts, pull up our socks, square our shoulders . . . and try to relax. Every one of you can make some contribution. I shall be giving you the address later. May I conclude by saying I laugh at those who say this country is struggling. Ha, ha, ha. We can turn the corner, if only we can find it. We will confound the Jonahs, the backsliders, the dismal Jimmies and the rest of our great people, and prove to the world that there are bigger, better, greater crises ahead. Good night.

BARRY CRYER

Alexander the Haigiographer

General Alexander Haig has contexted the Polish watchpot somewhat nuancely. How, though, if the situation decontrols can he stoppage it mountingly conflagrating? Haig, in Congressional hearings before his confirmatory, paradoxed his auditioners by abnormalling his responds so that verbs were nouned, nouns verbed and adjectives adverbised. He techniqued a new way to vocabulary his thoughts so as to informationally uncertain anybody listening about what he had actually implicationed. At first it seemed that the General was impenetrabling what at basic was clear. This, it was suppositioned, was a new linguistic harbingered by NATO during the time he bellwethered it. But close observers have alternatived that idea. What Haig is doing, they concept, is to decouple the Russians from everything they are moded to. An example was to obstacle Soviet ambassador Dobrynin from personalising the private elevator at Foggy Bottom. Now he has to communal like everybody else. Experts in the Kremlin thought they could recognition the word-forms of American diplomacy. Now they have to afreshly language themselves up before they know what the Americans are subtling. They are like chess grandmasters suddenly told to knight their bishops and rook their pawns. If that is how General

227

Haig wants to nervous breakdown the Russian leadership he may be shrewding his way to the biggest diplomatic invent since Clausewitz. Unless, that is, he schizophrenes his allies first.

THE GUARDIAN

Christmas Message
Margaret Thatcher

I'd like to take this opportunity to say a few Christmas words to all the young children who are expecting presents. Now, up till now I know these gifts have been given to you free of charge. But, good heavens, isn't it about time young people got a grip on reality and realised that we can't expect to jolly well get everything for nothing. So what we're going to do in future is ask all of you to pay for your presents at the market rate. It's not much to ask, and I think you'll find you appreciate a present much more when you've paid out hard cash.

PRIVATE EYE
Record: 'The Sound of Talbot'

Our Thrills in the Big Dipper

The Labour Government, 1964-1970. A Personal Record, *by J. Harold Wilson, is published jointly by Weidenfeld & Nicolson and Michael Joseph.*

I dictated a memorandum as we were being carried by the ratchet mechanism to the top of the first chute. I had long believed – and had said as much in a speech to the Wakefield Lads' Brigade on 17 June – that once we got to the top we should be able to see all that lay before us. It was the moment all of us in the cart had been waiting for, and the notes I had prepared were distributed, after I had made a few corrections to the typing, as we neared the summit. They were too late for the evening papers but with luck should be in plenty of time for the early editions next day. With only a few seconds to go before we were due to reach the crest of the rise Jim excitedly pointed out what had been obvious to me all along. We were not going to stay at the top for long. We were going to run helter-skelter down the other side. I told one of my staff to tell one of his staff to tell him on no account to panic. Everybody was watching us from the ground, and one ill-considered move would have been spotted and broadcast round the world. The message got through just in time and as we swooped down the chute. I dictated a minute bringing my previous memorandum up to date in the new circumstances with which we were suddenly faced.

As we came up the other side Roy was looking rather breathless. I asked him what was wrong. It appears his advisers had told him to lean against the pitch of the car as it took the 45-degree curve at the bottom. Had he leaned the other way he would, I think, have made a better run of it, but the advice he had received had resulted in his nearly being thrown out. Dick was darting to and fro and the car rocked from side to side. I felt strongly that there was only one course now open to us, but I called my colleagues together just as the car reached the top of the second chute. Should we get off or should we stay on board? Barbara, with her feminine intuition, said it was not possible to get off even if we wanted to, and I was very glad that somebody else had spoken my mind for me. It is much better that ideas should occasionally come from somewhere other than the chair. I looked around and nobody registered dissent. At this crucial moment in our journey we were united in our resolve to stay on board.

On the next ascent the machine made a louder clatter than usual, and by this time, although we were all thoroughly committed to what we were doing, one or two faces had begun to turn pale. One of my secretaries was shouting in my ear. I told him sharply that there was no need to raise his voice and asked what was the matter. He said the Duke of Montrose wanted to tell me a dirty joke. It was typical of the man that he should choose such a moment. I said, 'I see,' in a tone of voice which was meant to – and I think did – carry a wealth of meaning. But the laughter at this little sally was just subsiding when we suddenly reached the top of yet another chute. We were being thrown about in all directions and had to hold on to the very pound notes in our pockets. If we had lost our grip they would have fluttered away into the hands of people who had chosen the easier course of staying on the ground and who, as we had come to learn so well, would pounce on our money at the first opportunity. It was then that Roy, Jim, and I think Peter pointed to George who was gesticulating wildly from the ground hundreds of feet below. I had wondered where George was.

We had waited an hour and a half for him before coming on board. Evidently he had been detained. None of us could tell what he was saying, but one of the Downing Street staff who had been, and in many ways still was, a Boy Scout, remembered his semaphore and acted as interpreter. 'He's resigned,' he told me, and we buried our heads in our raincoats for the water chute . . . .

THE GUARDIAN

Strange
Meetings

Dylan Thomas's Pride and Prejudice

FIRST VOICE. It is night in the smug snug-as-a-bug-in-a-rug household of Mr and Mrs Dai Bennet and their simpering daughters – five breast-bobbing man-hungry tittivators, innocent as ice-cream, panting for balls and matrimony.

MRS BENNET. Our new neighbour, Mr Darcy, quite tickles my fancy.

MR BENNET. Don't let him turn Lizzy's head Darcy-versy.

ELIZABETH. I shall wed whom I please.

FIRST VOICE. And busy Lizzie retires to her room with visions of bridling up the aisle to 'I will' with half-a-dozen lovers. She dreams of coaches and pairs and being a fine lady; dressing for dinner in a silken gown and undressing afterwards for heaven knows what in the saucy haven of a double bed; swoons, seductions and *sal volatile;* tears, tantrums and tedium; the pettish petticoquettish world of the country-house marriage-go-round from which she and her whinnying sisterhood can never hope to escape.

STANLEY J. SHARPLESS

Jane Austen's Under Milk Wood

Captain Cat, of Schooner House, Llaregyub, in the county of Carmarthen, sat in his window-seat. His deficiency of sight being assisted by a liberality of percipience, he apprehended Mrs Ogmore-Pritchard with circumspection. Losing two husbands was no guarantee of her not hoping for a third and he envied neither Mr Ogmore nor Mr Pritchard their subservient roles. The ladies said that the Captain had only once considered marriage; the late Miss Probert was mentioned. But though he occasionally observed that Miss Price might pay more heed to the attentions of Mr Edwards, to their mutual advantage, he was more often heard criticising the imprudent Mr Waldo and the baneful Mr

233

Pugh and sympathising with their wives. He would never marry. The dissipations of this cheerful seaside village, with its luxuriant woody growths, and the constant memory of his wild days in the Navy, gave him sufficient pleasure.

LAURENCE FOWLER

Robert Lowell's Tyger

Tiger going like a flaming suppository
Through the black anus of the night,
What was the Lord God thinking of when he made you predatory?
Did He think He had the blue-print right?
With what foul magma did He light your eyes?
Or was it a meteor from unearthly skies,
Flashing above the stinking pits of hell?
Did the Lord God make the lamb as well?
And when He forged your sinewy heart,
Was He diverted by your roars?
Did He think the lamb would take it all in good part,
Bowels spilling out pinkly between your jaws?

T. GRIFFITHS

Death Again
Donne in the style of Betjeman

O John 'Doctor' Donne, O John 'Doctor' Donne,
The dance so soon over, the race nearly run;
In life's fearful twilight when Death lays his head,
You smile at the hourglass wherein falls the sand.
Can you be such a dreamer you fear not life's end?
Is it true that you look upon Death as a friend?
Are you right to insist your demise might be fun?
Or is it mere sophistry, John 'Doctor' Donne?

T. HOPE

234

P.G. Wodehouse's The Castle

K could see no glimmer of light in the situation. The Castle looked little better than a piece of ribbon development that had gone wrong, and a fat lot of good that was from the sightseeing point of view, so he toddled up to a cottage and heaved a snowball at a window.

'Well?' enquired a man with a beard not dissimilar in size or texture to a Nepalese prayer mat.

'I'd be awfully obliged if you could let me have a bit of sit-down,' K said soothingly, giving him the old oil. 'I'm the new land surveyor, don't you know.'

'Rrrr . . . .' breathed the old man through his lips that, like the Windmill, never closed.

K trickled in and sank into a chair.

'You can't stay here,' boomed a second man, with a smaller beard, resembling a startled hedgehog.

'Absolutely not!' K answered him. 'Just a spot of rest, what?'

T. GRIFFITHS

Joyce à Beckett

SAMUEL BECKETT was once JAMES JOYCE'S secretary. Is this how it went?

JOYCE. Take a letter *a latere dextro,* righthand shorthand lefthand. O calloo callay calligraphy, concatenate with curlicues and peripatetic pothooks, adorable mandoodling on the virgin page, blotting her nymphant shamus. To the Editor, *Transitions;* dear sir or madam, *re* Joyce in the lord, our reference your reverence (Father of) our latterletter. Pencilpoised, or tappingly trip, trippingly tap the tripewriter. *In principio erat verbum* –

BECKETT. There's no paper.

JOYCE. Ah, then it must be Sunday: we are depressed, but new-yorksunday is in his western high, or the heraldtribulation sings. See his glinting mirrormail farfreeglancing on the Horizon, see Cyril con a lea in the gardens of the west, later chronicletimes till the evening Star decline in the west, untergangler spengles his spangled miss under Standard rose by yonder burbling beaverbrook to follow her swannsong liederwriter.

BECKETT. There's no paper. Fogg said he would bring some. Many years ago. *There's no paper. Fogg, I said.* He may have gone to get some.

JOYCE. Which fog was that, witch? On a brumestick she strides the murky mistery of man, meaning awhirl in the blackdown blacknight freefall, her voicebells booming in the brumy air. O seasick omnes in that Void, wanton the fog to clearabell meaning!

BECKETT. Fogg went away. He may have gone to get paper. I don't know.

JOYCE. Then we'll skip the scratchpen scribbling, scratch our scribing. We'll use the obiterdictaphone, grave the word in a waxen image with our tapewriter electroloquacity. Marvellous mouthpiece into the vulvular valves and filigree filaments of it, the ambient lamps and lambent amps dancing a *coranto,* the English current jargoning into waxwords. Or tape, is it? Or wax *disce puer?* Er, h'rrrm, h'rrrm. Testing testing. To the Editor, *Transitions; re* Joyce in the lord, a greeting and message as it flies by my crow phone –

BECKETT. Some say that's a wax machine, some say it wanes. Or it may be tape, which is neither. But there's no tape, of course. Krapp took the last one. Ah, you can talk to that machine. I've talked to it for hours, for years. But it never says a thing back. Krapp, he knew how it worked. But he's gone. He knew where Fogg went, he went after him. Sometimes I think he left a message for me in that machine. Sometimes I look for paper myself (you remember, we wanted paper), sometimes I juggle the dials every which way on that machine, hoping for the voice of Krapp. Or Fogg.

As he twiddles the knobs on the machine there is a sudden burst of marvellous music from it.

JOYCE. O *sole mio tesoro, andante an Beatrice! O fatale Don Jove-annie Lauritz Melchoir*! Moomy minims, maximum clustercrotchets quavering in music's steepclouds! There's an errant clearabell voice clear and goldivox populi, arialleluias lovely in larynx of bassopranoperalto, heldentenor in a score of wunderbars riposting to a sweetish nightingale, with Orpheus O'Grady at the panharmonium and royalty in his red-plush stalls. Swooning sighstrings to his reedplaint till suddenly all's clear in a brassburst thunderclap on the lightning conductor of the bee bee sea seem funny orchestra.

BECKETT. That wasn't Fogg. Or Krapp. They weren't musicians.

JOYCE. Pigeonpost it then, a loftletter fluttering through chancy airs, highflown pigeonenglish by birdleg wing high o'er the western wave. To the Editor, *Transitions* –

BECKETT. You'd still want paper. There isn't enough here to go round a pigeon's leg. Fogg went to get paper, years ago. Every day since then I have wanted to write letters, marvellous letters. But there was no paper to write them on. Every day I sharpened my pencil some more, till now it's only a little bit of a thing. *(Shouting fiercely at sky:)* D'ye hear me? I'm here, waiting to write with me little bit of a pencil, before the stars go out.

JOYCE. We must wait till Fogg comes back.

Beckett stares at him.

No Fogg, no paper. It's a pity, though, that they weren't musicians, Fogg on the flute, Krapp on the violin. We'd hear their music, drawing nearer, as they came back, perhaps with paper . . . .

Pause.

BECKETT. Ah, and then what a stirring stringsong tirralee triumphonium, the fillfluter's divine windrush afflatus! Ah the fillharmonious ball of musicperforming writes of Springsong on the printemps page, tomtom the paper's sun went to bed with meaning's very self in a musicflash songburst –

JOYCE. *Here's* some paper. You write with your stylo, I'll write with mine.

PAUL JENNINGS

Rupert Brooke in the Style of McGonagall

Oh! if by any unfortunate chance I should happen to die,
In a French field of turnips or radishes I'll lie.
But thinking of it as really Scottish all the time
Because my patriotic body will impart goodness to the slime.
For I've been brought up by the bonnie country of Scotland
Which I like very much indeed with its lochs and plots of land
And many other picturesque sites which any tourist can see
So long as he is able to pay British Rail the requisite fee.

And you might give a thought too to my decomposing body
As it lies, poor dead thing, under the frog soddy.
For it will be thinking too of my very nice home country
And its weather which is anything but sultry,
And all the exceedingly jocund times I enjoyed there
And frolicked when I was able to in the soggy Scottish air.

J.Y. WATSON

Hercule Poirot Investigates an Elizabeth Bowen Novel

Poirot bowed courteously. 'It is *très gentil* of you to come and see me,
Mademoiselle,' he said.

Felicity felt glad she was wearing the stole; somehow its femininity
defied those very male moustaches.

'I had no alternative,' she answered.

'But surely, Mademoiselle, the alternative was – *ne pas venir, n'est-ce
pas?*'

'*Non!*' she replied sharply, deliberately asserting her own linguistic
powers. 'You see – if I had refused to come, it would have been
somehow, as it were, a confession of failure.'

'Confession! Then you confess, Mademoiselle? You killed your
lover, *c'est vrai?*'

'Confess, kill, lover,' she murmured. 'You use these words as though
they only had one meaning. But think how infinitely many gradations
of meaning there are to the word "lover" – '

'Enough! Mademoiselle, I do not tolerate the equivocation. I, Poirot, ask you the straight question. Did you or did you not murder Roderick Spencer-Poumphrey?'

'Does it matter?' she sighed.

'Matter? *Mon Dieu!* Do you suggest, Mademoiselle, that Death does not matter?'

'Oh, it matters in a sense, yes. But compared with the slow weariness of life, with the subtle degradations of years in which illusions, faith, hope, are gradually stripped away – does it really, perhaps, so very much matter?'

L. W. BAILEY

The Caretaker . . . Or Private Life

A basement. Dingy perhaps, but not actually dirty. Old furniture, but tastefully arranged. ASTON *is alone in the room; he wears an old leather jacket but well-cut trousers off which he's elegantly flicking the cigarette ash. (Nigel Patrick, perhaps?) Enter* DAVIES, *a tramp, but picturesquely dressed and with rather distinguished greying hair. (Wilfred Hyde White?)*

ASTON. Hello, matey, who are you?

DAVIES. I came, er, I come for my papers. Here, they said, or Sidcup.

ASTON. Very flat, Sidcup.

DAVIES. There's no need to be unpleasant.

ASTON. It was no reflection on the papers, unless of course they made it flatter. Do you come here often?

DAVIES. No, Budleigh Salterton, mostly. A better class of papers, there, and the moonlight on the bus-station roof is peculiarly attractive.

ASTON. Moonlight can be cruelly deceptive. How will you recognise it?

DAVIES. The moonlight?

ASTON. No, no, Sidcup.

DAVIES. There's bound to be a sign. If not, I shall ask. I'm told that people at bus-stations, if asked, often reply.

239

ASTON. In what?

DAVIES. English, mostly, or so they tell me: nowadays one must never be too hopeful.

ASTON. I remember a station. Long ago, it was, and terribly far away. Up north, well past Watford. Maybe even Berkhamsted. Or Bletchley. It was in the war – everyone terribly busy with rationing and rock cakes and killing Germans and dressing up in those funny tin hats and there, quite suddenly, unexpectedly, almost surprisingly, there was this woman. An ordinary, middle-aged woman, terribly ordinary and terribly, terribly middle-aged and with a funny sort of look in her eye as if she was really supposed to be wearing glasses. We knew at once, of course.

DAVIES. Knew?

ASTON. That we were terribly, terribly in love. (*He goes over to the piano, old but Bechstein, and starts to play softly.*) It was impossible, of course – too, too impossible for words and I suppose that was why we never actually spoke. Just stood there and stared and stared and wished the platform announcer could also have been to elocution classes. Then a train came – quite unexpectedly, really, out of a tunnel and with no sense of timing, and suddenly we knew it was all over. But sometimes, even now, I wake up in the night and wonder somehow if it could all have been different; if there hadn't been that awful fire at the Reichstag and then that common little man with the strange haircut shouting so much, would we have managed to speak? It all seems so terribly terribly sad and often, in the sudden chill of an autumn evening, or whenever Spring breaks through again, I know . . . .

DAVIES. A dark, secluded place, where no . . . .

ASTON. Did you say something?

DAVIES. No, no, I was just wondering about the papers and Sidcup and somehow everything seems so terribly complicated nowadays.

Enter MICK , younger than the other two, suave. Simon Williams perhaps?

MICK. You can't stay here: it's mine. Besides, who are you?

DAVIES. I'm Davies – there's an e before the last s. So important, don't you think? It makes me feel so terribly Welsh, and I always think that's what matters. It's no good feeling just a little bit Welsh.

MICK. What are you doing here?

DAVIES. I'm on my honeymoon.

MICK. Enjoying it?

DAVIES. It hasn't really started. What about you?

MICK. India, just back.

DAVIES. And the Taj Mahal, how was the Taj Mahal?

MICK. Incredible – a sort of dream. You'll have to go.

DAVIES. So you've said. It's just a question of the fare. Sidcup's not a day-excursion, whatever that might be. People seldom seem to come back.

MICK. Perhaps you'd better stay. I need a man to look after this place – is there anything you can do?

DAVIES. I play the piano a little, look rather good on balconies in evening dress, expanding cigarette holders, that sort of thing. What did you have in mind?

Curtain.

ALAN COREN

The Hawk in the Gutter

William Wordsworth's Immortality *in the style of Ted Hughes*

> Landscapes lie sullen;
> Scrublands, dank woods and hulking hills
> Menace me, annunciating madness,
> Just as they did when in dark ponds I fished
> For pike, immense, malevolent and old,
> Or hunted hares through vengeful thistle spikes
> In the blue summer air.

Shriek of torn flesh and grinding crunch of bone
Sing to me still.
Clouds, sick with sinister surgery, obscure
The sombre glint of the sun's eye,
Mocking the mutability of man,
His tiresome toils and toys.
In me the flower implants its poisoned dart,
Flushing my veins with a vile venom
Too deep for cleverness or care to cure.

ROBERT BAIRD

An Extravagant Fondness for the Love of Women

Strange, I thought the other day, when some persecuting critic explained to me that all modern academic novels were forged out of putting together C.P. Snow's Lewis Eliot with Kingsley Amis's Jim Dixon – strange that neither of these distinguished novelists actually recorded the occasion. Happily I was wrong, as this extract shows. I won't say which of the two did it; though the fact that it comes from a forty-volume roman-fleuve *called* Staircases of Disputation *may be a clue to some.*

A warm fire burned in my grate, its flicker illuminating the book-lined walls, as I sat in my Cambridge room that evening in the early Sixties – I am usually either sitting or eating when I begin a chapter. My fire, my leatherbound volumes, my warm body in the armchair formed a little pool of civilisation, though through the medieval wainscoting the draught from outside struck cold. Below, in the wintry courtyard, tourists with plastic cameras walked clumsily on the lawns, or kicked against buckets in the narrow Tudor passageways; being, however, from a lowly background, I felt this quite excusable. I could hear their murmurs of veneration for the ancient college, and realised how they would envy me my traditional rights and comforts, could they see me sitting there with the tray the gyp had left me, on it a decanter of nuts and a bowl of sherry. The rain rattled my windows. The leather-bound tome on my lap struck cold, or warm, I hardly remember which; after all, this is fifteen years ago. The book was a study of the Martyrdom of Polycarp, an old and well-loved interest of mine; and I was so deeply engrossed that I did not notice the step on my staircase, until someone knocked several times, with heavy knuckles, on my oak door.

'Come,' I called; and I looked up to see Dixon enter. The fire was, as I said, warm, the books radiant in its glow; but Dixon's entrance brought in the draught and wet of the weather outside, which struck cold into the room, and I hastily bade him shut the door.

'Well, wotcha, old sock,' he said, taking his place before my fire (not his fire) and warming his youthful, fleshless buttocks impetuously, 'I suppose this is what you call studying, then. Do a lot of that, do you?' As he spoke, his eyes flickered enviously over my ample chairs, my seventeenth-century tapestries, the rows of diaries, the volumes of briefs, the scientific notes, the political memoirs that betokened my eclectic interests; and his features assumed an expression which bore, I noticed, an extraordinary physical similarity to that of Dame Edith Sitwell . . . .

He produced, with a lithe movement, a small can of beer from the pocket of his turd-brown anorak and, from another of his many pockets, drew out a metal bottle-opener of the kind then recently introduced to facilitate this new fashion in drinking. With this, he succeeded in penetrating the circular container, and put it to his lips. It was not one of the more expensive or better reputed kinds of beer and he gulped it inattentively.

'I'm not disturbing you, am I?' he then went on, 'I see you're only reading. The kind of bloody boring stuff us chaps have to do to pretend we're up to something, eh, Lew?'

'One tries to keep up,' I said.

'Actually,' said Dixon, 'I hoped I'd catch you in. I wanted you to know that last evening I was accorded one of those there signal honours. In the election after dinner I emerged victor. I'm now captain of the darts team down the Feathers.'

'You know how delighted I am. Perhaps you'll allow me to present a bottle this evening, and record the occasion in the wine-book.'

Dixon sometimes gave the appearance of brashness, but I could see that he was taken right aback. He gave a shy, somewhat diffident smile. Down below in the court someone walked towards the chapel, whistling a passage of *Carmen*. Dixon seemed affected by this, and, as if to draw attention away from his embarrassed gratitude, he snatched up a small eighteenth-century alabaster figurine from my mantelshelf and crossed to the window. After a moment's pause, he opened the window, so that a draught of air struck cold to my chair, and hurled

243

out the precious object. The throw was evidently accurate; outside the music ceased, and a sailor's oath reminded me that Crystal had promised the Duke of Edinburgh as his guest at the feast that evening . . . .

MALCOLM BRADBURY

The Love Song of J. Omar Khayyam

Awake! for Morning in the Pan of Night
Has dropped the Egg that puts bad Dreams to Flight;
And Newspapers and empty Bottles gleam
Encircled by a Hangman's Noose of Light.

I sometimes think there's none so red a Nose
As when some *fin de siècle* Poet goes;
That every Hyacinth the Garden wears
Through a blank Pair of female Sockets blows,

Come fill the Tea-cups and the Ices bring
So little time to hear the Mermaids sing,
The Footman waits already with my Hat;
I shall be Seventy in the Fire of Spring.

The Moving Finger writes; and, having writ,
Some other Finger comes to cancel it,
And out of a single word and half a line
Makes Verses of profundity and Wit.

ROY FULLER